The Colours of Greater Manchester

Michael Eyre and Peter Greaves

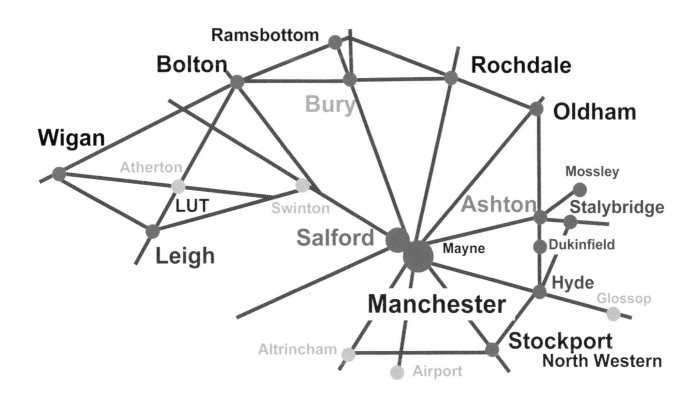

Capital Transport

First published 2009

ISBN 978-1-85414-329-7

Published by Capital Transport Publishing
PO Box 250, Harrow Weald, HA3 5ZH

Printed by 1010 Printing International Ltd.

© Capital Transport Publishing 2009

Acknowledgements

Much of the work for this book was done forty or fifty years ago – by the photographers. It is to them that the principal thanks and credit goes. Not just to those whose pictures appear in the book but to all who kindly searched their files to find slides and negatives for consideration. Many merited inclusion and it is only the constraint of the size of the book that precluded their use. We thank them all.

Particular gratitude is due to Monica Richardson for giving us continued access to the Photobus collection. The initial idea for this book arose before Arnold Richardson's untimely passing and Arnold spent many hours preparing slides. The directors of the Online Transport Archive ('OTA'), in particular Martin Jenkins, provided much material from their excellent collection, which includes the photographs of the late Reg Wilson and Jack Batty, and also gave freely of their time to search out specific pictures. Richard Morant deserves special mention for generously lending us parts of the splendid collection of his late brother Geoffrey, whose pictures are some of the best we have ever seen. David Beilby, Roger Davies, Geoff Burrows, Ted Jones, Mike Shaw and Harry Wall kindly gave their time to check facts, vehicle details and locations.

We have carefully recorded the photographers but if by some mischance a picture is wrongly attributed, we offer our apologies in advance. To anyone else who helped, named or not, our thanks.

COVER
This picture of Rochdale's Weymann-bodied Daimler Fleetline 325 and Bury's Weymann-bodied Leyland PD2 183 in Kay Gardens, Bury, captures the joint services that were at the heart of bus operation in the area that became Greater Manchester – for in Bury you could find the buses of more municipalities than any other town or city in the country, excepting Manchester. In addition to Bury's own fleet there were buses from Bolton, Manchester, Ramsbottom, Rawtenstall, Rochdale and Salford. There were two services between Bury and Rochdale – the 19 via Jericho and the 21 via Heywood. *May 1969, Geoffrey Morant*

Contents

Introduction

There was little local enthusiasm for the South East Lancashire and North East Cheshire Passenger Transport Executive ('SELNEC') taking over the bus operations of the local municipalities on 1st November 1969 and even less when it caused the break up of the North Western Road Car Company Ltd in 1972. The local government reorganisation of 1974 changed SELNEC into the Greater Manchester Passenger Transport Executive and, with equal lack of enthusiasm, Wigan Corporation's bus fleet was absorbed in 1974 and Lancashire United Transport Ltd in 1976.

A town or city bus fleet was a source of municipal pride, even rivalry; perhaps more important was the loss of local control of routes, services and fares. SELNEC was highly innovative in numerous aspects of organisation, operation and engineering; its more politically driven successor, Greater Manchester Transport, perhaps less so. True, there were many improvements but, with hindsight, most passengers felt the area was worse off.

So far as services were concerned, there was already very good, long-established inter-working and co-operation with a comprehensive network of jointly operated inter-town bus services that served the area with almost none of the artificial boundaries that sometimes existed in other towns. Some of these services were derived from the tramways but the majority had their roots in the co-ordinated network set up by the municipal and company operators in the late 1920s.

Each town or city had its own series of service numbers which meant that, across the area, some services had numbers which were duplicated. However most were well separated geographically and operated by differently coloured buses so that there was little confusion for passengers – certainly less than that from the wholesale renumbering of services that came with SELNEC.

We had better have a couple of pictures of sunglow orange SELNECs. Salford ordered 20 MCW-bodied Leyland Atlanteans to Manchester's 'Mancunian' design which were delivered new to SELNEC. 1204, which would have been Salford 327, outbound on Chapel Street having just left Victoria Bus Station. *September 1970, Roy Marshall*

The streets and roads were surely less attractive. Buses are a significant part of street furniture and their colourful liveries made an important contribution. Manchester buses were red, Salford's were green, Stockport's were red but a different shade from Manchester, Ashton's were blue, Rochdale's were blue too but a rich dark shade, Leigh's were a mid shade of blue, Oldham buses were crimson, Bury buses were pale green, Bolton's dark maroon, North Western's were red, and so on. This rainbow of colours disappeared into the sunglow orange and off white of SELNEC – cheerful enough in small doses but overpowering in quantity.

This book is a celebration of the bus fleets that disappeared – the corporations of Manchester, Salford, Ashton-under-Lyne, Bolton, Bury, Leigh, Oldham, Rochdale, Stockport and Wigan, the Stalybridge Hyde Mossley and Dukinfield Transport Board (SHMD), Ramsbottom Urban District Council, most of the North Western Road Car Company Ltd and Lancashire United Transport Ltd (LUT). Express services such as the X60 to Blackpool are excluded – they are part of a different story.

This is not a history book – the history is well covered elsewhere. It is a collection of fine colour pictures, selected on the basis that we liked them, taken in the late 1950s and 1960s by some of the best photographers. We have chosen the date SELNEC took over the municipal fleets as a rough cut-off. There isn't a picture of every type of bus from every fleet, although many are here.

In deciding the order of the operators in the book we have copied one of SELNEC's early and successful innovations. The Trans Lancs Express service started in January 1970 running hourly from Stockport, through Reddish, Denton, Guide Bridge, Ashton, Oldham, Rochdale, Heywood and Bury to Bolton. Worked by Ashton garage, it was at first operated with six of Manchester's Bedford VAL coaches. The journey time was one hour and 44 minutes and the end-to-end fare a remarkable 6 shillings (30p). It was not altogether a SELNEC idea, for although it only ran through the edge of what had been Manchester Corporation's territory (from Reddish to Guide Bridge), it was something that the Corporation had had in mind for some time. It therefore seemed to us that it would be a fitting acknowledgement of the old and the new that, having first covered the fleets of the two cities, the book should then more or less follow the route of the Trans Lancs Express.

In March 1970, the former Manchester Bedfords were replaced on the Trans Lancs Express by six of a batch of eight Plaxton-bodied Seddon Pennine IV coaches, 217-224. A relatively rare chassis, the Oldham-built Pennine IV had a forward-mounted Perkins 8.36-litre engine. 222 leaves Bolton's Moor Lane bus station on the 104-minute run to Stockport. After the fleets of the two cities, the order of the other municipalities in this book follows the route of the Trans Lancs round from Stockport. *August 1971, Roy Marshall*

Manchester

By a factor of four, Manchester Corporation Transport Department's fleet was the largest in the area that became Greater Manchester. From the day it was formed in 1900 the department never hesitated to go beyond the city boundary or arrange joint operation to provide efficient transport services.

In the late twenties it led the way in the introduction of a comprehensive and highly successful network of fast inter-town services; the operating and revenue sharing arrangements were 'a model for others to follow'. Supplemented by tram conversions this laid down a fine service network which was still in place when SELNEC took over.

From 1946 to 1966 conditions were such that the Department's flamboyancy of the 1930s seemed to give way to conservatism. This was not the case behind the scenes where much pioneering work was done. From 1966, style and innovation came to the fore again, especially with General Manager Ralph Bennett's trail-blazing Mancunians. Its name, too, was changed to Manchester City Transport.

Crossleys were a feature of the city's fleet but in 1947 Crossley Motors moved to a new works in Heaton Chapel, Stockport, a short distance outside the city boundary. Those few yards took away the firm's political leverage in the city and its hopes of continued business were further destroyed by its problematical post-war HOE7 diesel engine. Manchester then standardised on a fleet of Leylands and Gardner-engined Daimlers with Metropolitan-Cammell its preferred body supplier.

Asked to sum up Manchester Corporation Transport in a single phrase, a senior member of the bus industry said *'it was professional'*.

Manchester's pre-war 'Streamliners' were a feature of the city and so was the 'bus-a-minute' 53 service. One of the city's busiest, it followed a peripheral route, always about a mile from the city centre, from Cheetham Hill through Openshaw, past Belle Vue, through Rusholme to Brooks's Bar, Old Trafford or Trafford Park. This is Metro-Cammell/Crossley-bodied Daimler COG5 Streamliner 4259 at the Queens Road, Cheetham Hill terminus – 19 years old but still fully capable of a full turn on the arduous 53. *May 1959, John Kaye*

Its grey roof signifying that it is 7ft 6in wide, 1946 Crossley DD42 2919 is followed along Portland Street by brand new Leyland PD2 3592. In the background are two trolleybuses – an Ashton Crossley going to Ashton on the 219 and a Manchester BUT on the 218 to Stalybridge. 2919 and 3592 also have a trolleybus association, for they are working the cross-city services that replaced the Moston trolleybuses. *May 1959, John Kaye*

In the rebuilt Piccadilly bus station, Metro-Cammell-bodied Leyland PD1 3012, new 1947, waits to depart on the 64 to Heald Green – at the time only alternate journeys ran beyond Heald Green to Manchester's Ringway Airport. Jointly operated with North Western, for several years the route was restricted to 7ft 6in wide buses because of road width in Sharston – a slightly pointless restriction as it applied only to buses in service and the road was used by dozens of 8ft wide buses going to and from Manchester's Northenden garage. *June 1960, Geoffrey Morant*

Bus and building are of equal interest. The building is Lower Mosley Street bus station, opened in 1928. Terminus of almost all the express and long distance bus services into the city, it was jointly owned by a consortium of company operators including North Western, Ribble and LUT. The bus is Crossley DD42 2094 of 1948, its front mudguards cut back to help brake cooling. *June 1960, Geoffrey Morant*

Manchester United are at home and buses are summoned from all the garages to work the football specials to Old Trafford. On October 14th 1961, Queens Road garage's 1949 Metro-Cammell-bodied Leyland PD1 3119, on a 47x from Piccadilly, waits in the queue of traffic approaching Trafford Bar. The fans were in for a disappointment – Birmingham City won 2-0. *October 1961, John Ryan*

In 1964 newly spray-painted 1949 Crossley-bodied Daimler CVG5 4049 is at Exchange terminus, Deansgate, with the cathedral in the background. The hot paint spray finish saved money but quickly dulled and 4049 would soon lose its gloss. The area was much devastated by bombing in 1940, evidenced by the gardens and isolated building on the right of the picture. On the other side of the road North Western Leyland PD2 550 in-bound on joint service 3 from Flixton will turn right to reach its Cannon Street terminus. *August 1964, Ronald Barton*

There were fifty four of these all-Crossley trolleybuses – 1200-1237 were four-wheel TDD42, new 1949, and 1240-1255 were six-wheel TDD64, new 1951. Allocated to Hyde Road garage, they were first choice for the 210 service to Hyde. 1216 at the George Street, Piccadilly terminus. *Summer 1958, Don Jones*

Cannon Street bus station at ten minutes to three on a July Saturday afternoon in 1956. Manchester Leyland PD2 3246 is on the 63 to Heywood. New in 1951/52, 3200-3264's Metro-Cammell bodies were the last with Manchester's distinctive dipped window lines. Behind on the 17 is Rochdale's brand new Weymann-bodied Gardner-engined AEC Regent 285. Waiting to turn onto the 17 stand after 285 is a Manchester PD1 from the 3050-3099 batch on a 17x to Middleton; on the right is another PD1, from 3100-3199, the 4 to Bamford. *July 1956, Phil Tatt*

Along with 3200-3264, Metro-Cammell-bodied Daimler CVG6s 4100-4189 of 1950/51 were some of the best buses Manchester ever had and could be seen on main duties on trunk services for two decades. There were two orders, one for 50 and the second for 40 and they differed in detailed finish. On the cross-city 65 service, 4139 is at the Parker Street stop in Piccadilly bus station. An unusual occurrence is that the two middle sections of the paper advert for OMO washing powder have been put on in the wrong order. The advert should read 'OMO adds brightness'. 4139 will not carry the mistake for long – it is due for its second repaint which will be in the 'all-red' spray paint livery. *May 1960, Peter Roberts*

Although commonly used in the USA and Europe to indicate 'part route', use of an X-suffix to a service number was unusual in Great Britain. Manchester's 'X' evolved to mean a variety of things such as extra journey, route variation, short working or even a completely different service. In this case it indicated a works journey. 1953 Leyland-bodied PD2 3347 is on Oldham Road close to Droylsden Road, across from the department's Newton Heath office. About a mile away from the 53 route, it is going to Bradford Road and only about one third of its journey will be on the 53 proper. *June 1960, John Kaye*

Intended to be a clone of 4100-4189, 1953/54 Daimler CVG6s 4400-4479 looked very different with their so-called 'tin fronts' and flush-mounted windows. For many years they were the mainstay of the Wythenshawe services, as here with 4404 on the Piccadilly bus station stand for the 100 to Woodhouse Park. Its front mudguards have been cut back to provide better cooling for the front brakes. *July 1962, John Ryan*

Wythenshawe was mainly council housing but the Peel Hall estate on its eastern edge was privately developed and, as it grew, an all-day one-man-operated feeder service was introduced from the Benchill Hotel where passengers could transfer to a 100 or 103 to the city. Northenden garage's Northern Counties-bodied 1953 Leyland Royal Tiger 23, turns at Coleby Avenue. The 128 started in 1956 but it was 1966 before Peel Hall got an all-day service to the city. *June 1960, John Kaye*

To serve the city-owned international airport at Ringway, Manchester had a small fleet of coaches finished in blue. In 1953 it bought six Royal Tigers with bodies to the style of London Transport's airport coaches with a raised roof line and raised rear seating, allowing a huge luggage boot. Burlingham built 33-35 and provided frames for 30-32 which were finished by the Leestone Road, Sharston-based coachbuilder S H Bond Ltd. In the days when air travel was not for the masses, there was a dedicated coach for each flight and its indicators displayed the name of airline and destination. Coaches started from the luxurious city centre air terminal in the Royal Exchange buildings, St Ann's Square. This is Bond-bodied 31. *June 1960, Geoffrey Morant*

As air traffic grew, more coaches were needed and four Leyland Tiger Cubs, 36-39, were added in 1956, again with bodies by Burlingham. Different in body framing details from the Royal Tigers, they used up registration numbers which the department had had 'in stock' since 1953. 36-39 had oil-fired heaters to keep the coach warm whilst standing at the airport, the department claiming it was the first use of these. 38's driver stands smartly upright, ushering his passengers onto the coach. *June 1960, Geoffrey Morant*

24 and 25 were Leyland Royal Tigers new in 1953 with Northern Counties 'crush loader' bodies. With a wide centre entrance and large central standing area they could carry some 60 passengers, just under half having to stand. Little surprise they proved unpopular with crews and passengers alike and were converted to normal seating. When withdrawn they were passed to Ringway airport for airside use. Shortly after its conversion, 24 is in Chorlton Street in 1960 and, 12 years later, on the apron at Ringway along with British European Airways Viscount G-AOHJ and Aer Lingus BAC 1-11 EI-ANG. *July 1960 and August 1972, Geoffrey Morant*

Manchester's trolleybus system faded away over the years 1955 to 1966. Stevenson Square was the terminus of the 211 Moston via Oldham Road, converted in 1955, and the 215/216 Audenshaw/Ashton/Stalybridge services which were the last to go in 1966. In this picture, conversion of the 215/216 has started. Sandwiched between Burlingham-bodied BUT 1316 of 1955 on the 215x and the arriving 1323 on a 216 is a Leyland-bodied PD2 diesel on the 215. Stevenson Square was also terminus for the motor bus services to Oldham. Metro-Cammell-bodied PD2 3572 is on the stand for limited stop service 2 to Chadderton, Shaw and New Hey. *Mid 1966, Howard Piltz*

With a growing need to reduce costs, there was a move towards lighter buses and Daimlers 4510-4549 new in 1956/57 had Gardner 5LW engines and Northern Counties lightweight bodies. 4510 is on service 12 – the Flixton services (3, 5, 11, 12 and 23) were all worked jointly with North Western. Behind, on service 5, is 1949 Daimler CVG5 4004. It, too, had a 5LW engine but its heavy body was the exact opposite of that on 4510 and 4000-4099 were amongst the most underpowered buses ever. *October 1961, John Ryan*

A brand new Manchester bus, resplendent with shiny black mudguards, dark brown lining between the red and cream side panels and no side advertisements; even the 'Leyland' badge on the radiator is picked out in red. 3471-3520 were Leyland PD2s with bodywork built in Blackpool by Burlingham. Parrs Wood garage's 3498 of 1958 is on the Gatley stand in Piccadilly bus station. A 'maker's error' was the number plate on the radiator grille – Manchester's specification called for it to be on the bodywork so that grilles damaged in service could easily be replaced. A note was sent to Burlingham and 3502 onwards conformed. *February 1958, Geoffrey Morant*

4550-4579 were Daimler CVG6s with similar Burlingham bodies to the fifty Leylands. They had a smaller, simpler radiator cowl, developed by Manchester and Daimler to reduce the cost of accident damage and improve the driver's view of the kerb. On a Metro-Cammell Orion body it married happily with the body styling, but the result on these Burlinghams was a mish-mash of uprights and curves, square and rounded corners. Outbound from Stevenson Square, 4571 leans as it enters Oldham Street. The bus has been repainted into the drab 'all red' and fitted with a replacement front grille. *Roy Marshall, September 1968*

15

3543 pulls away from the Lower Mosley Street bus station stop. Central Station is on the other side of the road. Fifty years on, the Bridgewater Hall is on the site of the bus station, Central is the city's exhibition centre and trams run where the advertisement hoardings were. 3521-3620 were Leyland PD2s with Metro-Cammell bodies. 3543, new in October 1958, was one of the last Manchester buses to be painted in the 'proper' livery. *May 1959, John Kaye*

Thunder clouds. After having to keep them in store at Northenden garage for almost five months whilst an agreement for their use was negotiated with the union, Manchester got 3621-3630, its first (and early) examples of the rear-engined Leyland Atlantean into service in April 1960 on service 101 to Wythenshawe. Appropriately in this June 1960 picture, the thunder clouds have passed and the sun catches 3624 as it passes 1939 Leyland TD5 3939 standing in the bus lay-by on Princess Road just before Barlow Moor Road. Still in smart condition, the TD5 would serve for another year. *June 1960, John Kaye*

Fog. The word on the intermediate blind on Daimler Fleetline 4620 inbound on London Road, approaching Fairfield Street junction, seems to be stating the obvious. However the dense fogs of the 1950s and early 1960s often did not extend to the suburbs and the display gave warning of disruption to passengers waiting there. This is the only picture we have ever seen of it in real use – more often it was set by a humorous crew either for amusement or as a comment about management. *Winter 1964, Howard Piltz*

Below Bus stop signs were not Stockport's greatest strength. You would be right to be puzzled by this 'Bus Stage' sign with a 'Bus Stop 92' a few yards behind it at the Rising Sun, Hazel Grove, Stockport – and you would be in for a disappointment if you stood at the wrong one. And more so, for just behind the photographer there was another 'Bus Stop' sign with 'North Western' on it but no service numbers. The latter was for the purely North Western services such as the 27 from Buxton. The yellow Bus Stage was for the 20/20A joint Manchester / Stockport / North Western limited stop from Woodford and Poynton, whilst the '92' one was the terminus at the time of the 92 and should have been a Bus Stage. Two week-old Manchester CVG6 4639 and a Stockport Leyland on the 92. *Late 1963, Ian Stewart*

With the growth in airport traffic and an increase in private hire, 1962 Park Royal-bodied Leyland Tiger Cubs 51-60 were in airport livery. Known as 'the blue singles' they had coach seats and luggage boots but were used on normal services when not required for private or airport work. 54 is leaving the airport for Chorlton Street – the green double-decker in the background is a Crosville Bristol Lodekka on a private hire. *July 1967, Reg Wilson*

Produced to meet Manchester's requirement for a shorter bus when industry opinion was moving towards high-capacity single-deckers, the Leyland Panther Cub was 33ft long rather than the Panther's 36ft. The department bought twenty, numbered 61-80, with Park Royal bodies. Before entering service 76 was used by Leyland for demonstration to potential customers, visiting Southport, Lancaster, Bury, Chesterfield and Leigh. Here it is at Kew, Southport. *May 1965, Roy Marshall*

On Chapel Street and approaching Salford's Victoria Bus Station, Manchester Daimler 4717, its windows plastered with traffic notices, on the joint cross-city service from Whitefield to East Didsbury, contrasts with Salford Leyland PD2 239. Both entered service in 1966. The Metro-Cammell body was plain and Manchester had some improvements made to its frontal appearance with the moulded front panel and curved windscreen, although the latter was more in the interests of driver's vision. The keyboard visible in the Volkswagen's rear window is evidence of Manchester's association with the pop music culture that fuelled much change in the 1960s. *June 1966, Geoffrey Morant*

In 1965 Ralph Bennett succeeded Albert Neal as Manchester's general manager. Previously at Bolton, he did more than most to improve the appearance of the United Kingdom's buses. The change is shown starkly in this picture of two month-old MCW-bodied Leyland Panther 99 outside the Queens Hotel in Portland Street along with 1958 PD2 3540, a Fleetline and, in the background, a 1953 Northern Counties-bodied Leyland PD2. The crews were still careless at blind settings however – a 219x went nowhere near Culcheth Lane. *July 1967, Roy Marshall*

Ken Mortimer of the Department's staff designed what he considered a modern bus. His manager showed the drawings to Ralph Bennett who promptly adopted it. With the coming authorisation of one-man operation, the department's engineers decided upon wide dual doorways to speed passenger flow and a high standing capacity. So was born Manchester's new bus – the 'Mancunian'. In accord with Manchester policy, the first order was divided equally between Leyland and Daimler. The bodies were by Park Royal – a new supplier for Manchester's double-deckers. Leyland Atlantean 1018 is seen on its first week in service. *April 1968, Roy Marshall*

The 1969 Mancunians were to the maximum length of 33 feet, the order again divided equally between Leyland and Daimler. MCW won the body contract but was busy and sub-let it to Park Royal. The clever black and yellow logos on the front of the bus indicated coin-in-the slot fare collection – in this case supplemented by a driver's Setright ticket machine for passengers without change. In the George Street section of Piccadilly Bus Station, Daimler Fleetline 2080 loads for Baguley Hospital – originally a small sanatorium at the end of a country lane, it would become the Wythenshawe Hospital complex of the 21st century. *May 1969, Geoffrey Morant*

At Bolton Ralph Bennett built up a good relationship with East Lancashire Coachbuilders and its bodies had a fine reputation. Winning an order from Manchester against the mighty Park Royal and MCW was nevertheless a feather in the firm's cap and, before placing the order, Ralph Bennett was at some pains to confirm that the firm would make a profit (which it did) and was not 'buying the order'. Of the twenty four that East Lancs built, twelve had single doors. 1969 Leyland 1138 is on inter-suburban service 7 at Brookdale Park, Newton Heath. *1969, Ronald Barton*

A fleet of twelve modern luxury coaches was introduced for airport and private hire work, the plan being to replace six each year. They were Bedford VALs with Plaxton coach bodies, finished in a smart new livery of white and turquoise blue. The first of the second six, 207, new in 1968, is seen arriving at Chorlton Street on the airport service with an SHMD Fleetline also bound for Chorlton Street in the background. *September 1968, Roy Marshall*

A Mayne & Son Ltd

In the 1930s, 1940s, 1950s and 1960s a small independent operator working a busy local service into the centre of a major city was very unusual - but Arthur Mayne was very very independent. For forty years he successfully resisted Manchester's attempts to buy him out and, probably because government mandarins overlooked small private firms, Mayne didn't go into SELNEC. Indeed, as soon as SELNEC introduced its orange and white livery, Mayne buses were smartly painted into something like Manchester's red and cream.

Until then Mayne's buses were maroon and pale blue. Mainly AECs, they were about as different from the corporation's as could be and were very much a part of the Ashton New Road, Clayton and Droylsden scene.

Mayne ran two services. The principal one – a limited stop – ran from Dale Street in the city centre, out through Clayton, passing his garage on Ashton New Road, and Droylsden to Audenshaw, where it terminated at Kershaw Lane. The second service was a local feeder from the trolleybus terminus on the city boundary at Edge Lane to Sunnyside Road on the Greenside estate. In 1958, after careful negotiation, the latter was joined with the corporation's service to Edge Lane to provide a limited stop from Sunnyside Road to Stevenson Square, worked jointly with the corporation until the abandonment of the trolleybuses when its operation became exclusively Mayne.

Mayne outlasted everyone else in this book. It was 2008 before the much-expanded stage service business passed to Stagecoach.

Weekdays to Kershaw Lane, summer weekends to Blackpool sums up the work of KNA 877, one of a pair of AEC Regent III with East Lancs bodies new in 1949. The small green light by its indicator was to identify a Mayne's bus from a corporation one at night – there were far more obvious differences. Two of Mayne's red and cream coaches are in the background at Mayne's garage on Ashton New Road, Clayton. *Summer 1959, Peter Roberts*

6972 ND was one of three AEC Regent V new in 1961 with Park Royal bodies of a design that must rate as one of the ugliest. The bus is at the Stevenson Square terminus of the service to Sunnyside Road – joint with Manchester but wholly operated by Mayne's after 1966. *September 1970, John Kaye*

Below 1965 AEC Regent V CXJ 521C with a stylish East Lancs body built by East Lancs' associate Neepsend, on Mayne's original service, from Dale Street in the city to Kershaw Lane, Audenshaw. The bus is outbound on Newton Street, about to turn right into Great Ancoats Street. A few barrels of Wilson's best are being delivered to the Britannia pub, watering hole for workers at the Royal Mail's main sorting office next door. *June 1966, Geoffrey Morant*

Salford

The word that describes Salford's post-war fleet of some 320 buses is 'immaculate'. It was not always so, for at the end of the war its buses were in dreadful condition and how new general manager Charles Baroth rapidly achieved so dramatic a change is well recorded elsewhere. A new livery of dark green and primrose distinguished its buses from those of Manchester and this, and the 195 Daimlers built to Charles Baroth's exacting specification, became almost as much a symbol of the city as its coat of arms.

The boundary between Salford and Manchester ran almost through the city centre. Proud as Salford and its general manager were, they were aware of their market and Salford's buses showed 'MANCHESTER' as the destination on the inter-town limited stop services from Warrington, Wigan, Leigh and Bolton, even though their terminus was just inside Salford. Geographically correct was its use on the local services that terminated in King Street West off Deansgate, which actually was a couple of hundred yards inside Manchester.

Arising from disputes over the tramways in the early 1900s, for years the two cities' transport departments had barely been on speaking terms with the result there was no cross city working between them. Charles Baroth tackled this, too, and joint 57/77 Reddish – Swinton and 95/96 East Didsbury – Whitefield services were introduced.

Long after side and rear advertisements were carried on the buses of every other operator in the area, Salford's remained unsullied by such things until after Charles Baroth retired in 1965.

Salford City Transport had class.

This picture of Victoria Bus Station captures Charles Baroth's Salford. Neatly parked at their stands, with indicators correctly set, are two of his 195 Metro-Cammell-bodied Daimlers, a nicely turned out Morris traffic van (certainly not there for breakdowns), an AEC Reliance single-decker and, in the background a new Leyland PD2. Even the van had a registration number to match its fleet number. The coat of arms was moved to the upper deck side panels in 1951 – a Baroth ruse when a councillor suggested Salford should have adverts on the side of its buses.
1964, Peter Roberts

The legacy of orders from the previous regime showed its lack of direction – 16 Crossley DD42 with 8.6 litre engines, 15 AEC Regent III with 9.6 litre engines and 18 Leyland PD1 with 7.4 litre engines, all with Metro-Cammell bodies and 17 more PD1s with Leyland bodies. All were planned to have only 50 seats but Charles Baroth had most changed to 54 or 56 before delivery. This is 1947 AEC Regent 273. The Regents were not over popular with him – 'too powerful, too thirsty' – but he ran them in service until 1962. *1960, Peter Roberts*

Leyland-bodied PD1 309 pulls away from Pendleton Church on service 50. The area across the road behind the bus is of transport interest. The low, pale red-coloured building that can just be seen to the rear of 309 is the showroom and offices of Foster and Seddon Ltd, builders of Seddon trucks. Behind it used to be the Pendleton works of the Manchester Carriage and Tramways Company, which operated the two cities' horse trams, many of which were built there. *1961, Reg Wilson*

At a time when Salford was desperately short of good buses, a cancelled export order for 30 Leyland-bodied Leylands was snapped up. Intended to be PD2s with the O.600 9.8 litre engine, Salford had them changed before build to 7.4 litre-engined PD1s. As time passed the durability and reliability of the O.600 more than offset the fuel saving of the smaller engine but this was not known in 1948. One of the last to retain the silver roof version of the green livery, 316 is in Victoria Bridge Street at the side of the bus station. *May 1959, John Kaye*

Charles Baroth's masterpiece was the fleet of 195 Daimler CVG6s with Metro-Cammell bodies. Always maintained in splendid condition, not even a murky day could dull their gloss. Salford fitted a red dome between the front upper-deck windows to indicate an 8ft-wide bus. After what was always a brisk journey on limited stop service 8 (11 heavily-trafficked miles in 38 minutes), 462 is in Trinity Street, Bolton, almost at the Thynne Street terminus. Trinity Street station is on the left of the picture and Bolton Parish church on the right. *July 1955, Phil Tatt*

The CVG6s were still in fine fettle in 1963, and 517 is in Portland Street, Manchester on joint cross-city service 95/96 which ran from East Didsbury to Whitefield. *1963, Photobus*

441-455 were to have been Burlingham-bodied CVG6 single-deckers but this plan was revised in 1950 when approval was given for the operation of service 6 (Eccles – Swinton – Prestwich – Radcliffe) by 7ft 6in-wide double-deckers – the single-deck restriction was not due a low bridge but to the then steep and twisting Rainsough Brow, Prestwich. 452-455 were altered to have 7ft 6in wide double-deck bodies to Salford's specification. 455 is seen at the King Street West terminus just off Deansgate, Manchester. The store across the road is the famous Kendal Milne's – Manchester's equivalent of Harrods. *July 1964, Ronald Barton*

With its fleet renewed, Salford needed no more new buses for ten years. Fifty arrived in 1962, including Weymann-bodied AEC Reliance single-deckers 102-110. 104 is on Chapel Street having just left Victoria bus station on a Sunday afternoon. Service 5 was the only Salford service that actually needed single-deckers because of a low bridge – the one under the Bridgewater canal in Barton Lane, Eccles. *May 1962, Geoffrey Morant*

111-140 were Metro-Cammell-bodied Daimler CVG6s with conventional rear platforms. In-bound from Peel Green, Eccles, 126 is passing the end of Blackfriars Road. On the left side of Blackfriars Road, immediately beyond the railway bridge, was an office and a tiny yard, in which there would usually be a second hand bus. Modest it was but this was the headquarters of Frank Cowley, one of the biggest dealers in used buses. His Rolls-Royce, registered FC 7, would be parked somewhere close by. Cowley had large storage yards at Moseley Road, Fallowfield; Clifton Road, Prestwich and Pennington, Leigh – the latter often with over a hundred used buses. *May 1962, Geoffrey Morant*

The last six of the CVG6s, 141-146, had front-entrance bodies. Here 145 pulls out of the dank gloom of Greengate bus station. Just across the road from Victoria, Greengate was the terminus of the limited stop services to Warrington (10), Bolton via Little Hulton (12), Worsley (23), Leigh (26), Westhoughton, Wigan and Liverpool (32,38,39) and some local services. It was nothing more than a very long railway bridge under Exchange Station, with bus stops and simple barriers. Dirty water dripped from the roof; the street lighting was always on. It was a thoroughly miserable place. *October 1962, Roy Marshall*

To gain experience with rear-engined buses, there were two each of Daimler's Fleetline (147/48) and Leyland's Atlantean (149/50), with off-the-shelf Metro-Cammell bodies on which the cream was reduced to a single band. The background to this picture of 150 at Worsley terminus is, therefore, much more interesting than the bus. The half-timbered building is the 1849 Court House; behind it is the Bridgewater Canal and the entrance to the Duke of Bridgewater's coal mines. Opened in 1765, the canal brought cheap coal into the city and was a key factor in the industrial growth of Manchester and Salford. There were also swift passenger boats to Manchester – journey time 2½ hours, fare 1 shilling in 1765, down to 3 pence first class, 2 pence second by 1843. A trip to Piccadilly on 150 in 1963 took 38 minutes and cost 1s 1d. *March 1963, Roy Marshall*

The ubiquitous Leyland PD2 arrived very late in Salford in 1963, just as Manchester was awaiting its final ones. A fleet of 103 was built up, intermixed with Atlanteans, a few Fleetlines and a couple of Daimler CCG6s which had constant mesh gearboxes and were much disliked by drivers. 239 was one of twenty five PD2s delivered in 1966. A particular feature of Charles Baroth's Salford buses was the framework which brought the handles for the indicators down to a level where they could be reached by crews standing on the ground – 'no excuse for blinds not set correctly'. *April 1966, Geoffrey Morant*

Manchester also tried the constant mesh gearbox Daimler CCG6. It bought five in 1963 but drivers at the 'Daimler' garages (Princess Road, Northenden and Birchfields Road) refused to drive them. 4650-54 were sent to Queens Road, a 'Leyland' garage where the crews were well used to the constant mesh box of PD1s. On Cheetham Hill Road, 4652 on limited stop 4 to Bamford follows Salford 253 on the 35 to Bury on a miserably wet day. *1966, Ronald Barton*

Salford's new buses in 1968 and 1969 were Leyland Atlanteans – 283-303 of 1968 had MCW bodies but Park Royal won the order for the 1969 batch, 304-323. One imagines that by-then-retired Charles Baroth would have had something to say about Park Royal's ugly design. The firm tried to inflict it on Manchester when it won the order for the Mancunians, receiving a short, blunt reply from Ralph Bennett. 302 is leaving Victoria with a Manchester PD2 on the joint 95/96 in the background, and, almost at the same point but facing the opposite direction, 307 is turning into Victoria Bridge Street. *September 1969, Reg Wilson and Roy Marshall*

Stockport

Anything to do with buses in Stockport has to start at Mersey Square in the town centre. If you stood in the middle of the square in the 1950s and 1960s and looked towards Manchester, as in this picture, you would see lots of Stockport buses with maybe a Manchester or a North Western. Turn around and face towards Hazel Grove and there would be more or less the opposite – lots of North Westerns. Facing the camera are Stockport's East Lancs-bodied PD2s 49, 28 and 46. On the right of the picture construction has started of the Merseyway shopping precinct. *April 1967, Reg Wilson*

By any standards of financial or other measure, Stockport's transport department was of the best. The fleet of around 170 buses was nicely turned out, it provided good services and low fares and used its money prudently.

It achieved this by staying with proven designs and methods, and caring for its fleet. Both its garages were in the town centre – in Mersey Square and just across the road at the corner of Wellington Road and Heaton Lane. When town centre redevelopment took these sites, a splendid new garage and works were built a couple of hundred yards away in Daw Bank, just behind the railway viaduct. It was opened in January 1968

To take a minor example of Stockport's standards, if you looked into Heaton Lane or Daw Bank, there would be a neatly parked line of identical Leylands with their front ends lined up to within an inch or so.

Stockport was a Leyland fleet. Politics caused it to take post-war Crossleys and wartime restrictions the utility Guys, but having got them it looked after them and got a full service life. Then came the fleet of East Lancs-bodied Leyland PD2s and PD3s which must rank amongst the best looking buses ever made. They were enhanced by a traditional livery of red and white with beading picked out in black, which remained unchanged by passing fashions until the final new buses before SELNEC took over.

Stockport was good.

Stockport 175 is in fine condition in Heaton Moor Road on a short to the Manchester boundary at Parrs Wood. New in 1936, 171-178 were Leyland TD4c with Leyland bodies. The 'c' suffix to the chassis type indicated torque converter transmission. Popular for a time in the 1930s, as it more or less removed the need for gear changing, making it easier for tram drivers to move over to bus work, it had several shortcomings not least being high fuel consumption. Most operators replaced it with a conventional gearbox and Stockport did so in 1947, although the redundant torque converter header tank was left in place on the nearside front bulkhead. *April 1959, John Kaye*

There were twenty of these English Electric-bodied Leyland centre-entrance single-deckers, new in 1936/37 for the jointly operated inter-town limited stop services from Manchester. Until the war and shortly after, almost all these services were single-deck operated. Those through Stockport were the 18 (Dialstone Lane), 20 (Poynton/Woodford), 33 (Romiley) and 74 (Vernon Park via Cheadle). The 75 (Green End, Burnage – Stockport – Offerton) service was also single-deck. Pre-war the plan was to extend it to Manchester and interwork with the 74, hence its Manchester series number. This never happened but by some quirk the 75 continued to be single-deck and to show Manchester's X suffix on short workings. Leyland TS7 192 in Mersey Square. *April 1963, Roy Marshall*

Stockport was allocated sixteen wartime Guy Arabs with Massey bodies. Delivered in 1943/44/45 they had registrations from the long block of numbers which the corporation was allocated in 1936 – it took ten years for the block to be used. The bodies were rebuilt in 1950/51, unusually keeping their original details apart from the wooden slatted seats, and all ran until 1963/64 by which time they were a rare reminder of wartime austerity. 224, the last of the batch, is seen in Mersey Square. *May 1960, John Kaye*

After the war Stockport built up a fleet of 65 Crossley DD42s, all but one against the wishes of its management. One (207) was owed from a pre-war 'trial' order for three Mancunians of which only two had arrived. Newly overhauled, its paintwork gleaming, 227 climbs the short steep brow from Mersey Square to St Peter's Square passing the offices of the local paper. It was one of twenty with Manchester-style Crossley bodies allocated to Stockport by the government and delivered in 1946. The other 44 were the result of Crossley Motors' move from Gorton, Manchester, to Heaton Chapel which ended Manchester's 'local industry' support for Crossley. Instead the firm successfully applied political pressure to Stockport's council. *May 1959, John Kaye*

There is more to this 1957 picture of the Manchester terminus of trunk 92 service to Stockport and Hazel Grove than first meets the eye. The new section of road surface bottom left of the picture is part of the works for the new Piccadilly Bus Station and one-way system, opened in 1958. The 92 terminus has moved temporarily to this stand in Parker Street at the side of the car parks, effectively created by the wartime bombing of 1940, on which construction of Piccadilly Plaza would soon commence. The two Stockport Leyland-bodied PD2s are in 'as new' condition, with the old style fleet number transfers used by Stockport from 1929 to 1957. *Autumn 1957, Phil Tatt*

On a bright sunny day, newly repainted 282 makes the 180 degree turn from Mersey Square onto Wellington Road South on a short working 92X to Hazel Grove. The buildings behind the bus will later be replaced by the new Merseyway precinct, and the shops at the near end of Princes Street, on the left of the picture, by the new Debenham's store. *May 1959, John Kaye*

35

Things look less inviting when the day is damp and overcast. A Stanier 'Black Five' locomotive takes a short goods train across Stockport viaduct, one of the largest brick structures in Western Europe. A North Western Bristol K5G and Fleetline and a corporation Leyland are on the stands outside the North Western office as Crossley DD42 316, one of the final batch which had the improved 'downdraught' engine, climbs out of Mersey Square en route to Adswood. Numbered 309-332 they were new in 1951 and withdrawn in 1967/68. *1966, Ronald Barton*

There was a gap of seven years before the next new buses arrived and they were Stockport's first 8ft wide ones. New in 1958, 333-342 were Leyland PD2s with Crossley bodies on Park Royal frames. Already almost fully loaded, 341 waits behind a Manchester Northern Counties-bodied Daimler CVG5 in Piccadilly, Manchester to pull onto the stop outside Woolworth's. A fruit seller's barrow stands at the corner of Oldham Street – these barrows were a feature of Piccadilly for years. The football window bill on the upper deck of 341 is for Stockport County's home match with Oldham Athletic on 23rd March 1963. Stockport won 2-1. *March 1963, Roy Marshall*

The 1958 vehicle intake also included four Leyland Tiger Cubs, again with Crossley bodies on Park Royal frames. In Mersey Square, 403 leaves the stand in front of the Plaza cinema. Comparing this picture with that of the wartime Guy shows that furniture removers Ormesher's, which owned the imposing brick warehouse and repository next to the Plaza, had been taken over by national firm Pickford's. *April 1969, Roy Marshall*

The choice of bodybuilder for the 1960 Leyland PD2s was unusual. Longwell Green Coachworks was based in the Bristol suburb of that name and had close associations with bus builder Bristol. Its price was the lowest but there was more than that to the choice – Stockport general manager E B Baxter commented privately that he recommended them because he knew the firm would do the high quality job he wanted. Numbered 343-352 their styling was neat yet individual. 352 is in Ashton bus station on the joint Ashton, SHMD, Stockport service to Hyde and Stockport with two SHMD Fleetlines and an Ashton Atlantean. *March 1969, Geoffrey Morant*

Stockport chose East Lancashire Coachbuilders for its future bodywork including that on Leyland PD2s 353-362 which arrived in 1962. 356 along with Manchester Royal Tiger 3 and PD2 3652 is in Manchester's Chorlton Street bus station. Built in 1958 to relieve congestion at Piccadilly, Chorlton Street was depressingly located amidst decaying warehouses on a vacant site about 250 yards down Portland Street – just far enough to be really inconvenient. Limited stop services to Stockport, Poynton/Woodford, Dukinfield, Alderley/Macclesfield, Bramhall, Romiley, Glossop and the airport service moved there. This version of Chorlton Street was unwelcoming enough but behind the Manchester double-decker there are signs of what was to follow – a bleak multi-storey car park with the bus station on its gloomy, draughty and dirty ground floor. It rivalled Salford's Greengate. *May 1962, Geoffrey Morant*

Stockport's fleet numbering restarted at 1 with ten more PD2s similar to 353-362. Subsequent deliveries reverted to the traditional radiator grille and the result was a very handsome bus. 11-25 were new 1964, 26-40 followed in 1965 and 41-70 in 1967, half of the latter having bodies built in Sheffield by East Lancs' associated Cravens-group company Neepsend. 38 is in Mersey Square on a 17x to Longford Road West in Reddish with two others in the background. *April 1969, Roy Marshall*

The 1968 delivery was fifteen 30ft-long Leyland PD3s, 71-85. Similar 86-97 followed in 1969, the last six having front-entrance bodies. On Chorlton Street, Manchester, having just left the bus station, 93 is approaching Whitworth Street, named after Stockport-born Sir Joseph Whitworth, whose screw thread became one of the first national standards. His substantial engineering factory was in Openshaw, next door to the works of Crossley Brothers. Whitworth gave generously to the area, founding the University of Manchester Institute of Science and Technology, Stockport Technical College and the Whitworth Art Gallery. *September 1969, Roy Marshall*

With the end of production of front-engined double-deckers, Stockport had to buy rear-engined ones and 98-107 were to have been East Lancs-bodied Bristol VRs. A disastrous fire at East Lancs' works destroyed them before completion; the fire-damaged chassis were sold by the insurers and exported to Australia. Their livery has been a matter of minor speculation as to whether it would have matched that of 1968 East Lancs-bodied Leyland Leopard single-deckers 404-408. 404 passes the telephone exchange on appropriately named Exchange Street, the new route into Mersey Square opened when right turns from Wellington Road South were banned. *October 1969, Geoffrey Morant*

NORTH WESTERN

Slightly cheeky, always cheerful and a wonderfully loyal staff described the North Western Road Car Company Ltd. Its buses seemed to go faster than those of the corporations and, although its fares were sometimes higher and its staff less well paid, people liked North Western.

Established in Macclesfield, in 1924 it moved to Charles Street, Stockport. Squeezed on all sides by corporation transport departments, against all logic it expanded, strenuously defending its territory against municipal operators from Warrington through Stockport round to Rochdale, not least the giant Manchester Corporation. Its most crucial move – and a brave one – was to gain lucrative access to the centre of Manchester by joining the municipal limited stop bus scheme of the late twenties as a full partner.

Its operations in Cheshire, Derbyshire and Staffordshire were largely single-deck but in Greater Manchester North Western was about double-deckers and we focus upon these in the pictures.

When it came to its fleet of over 500, North Western liked Bristols, continuing to buy them after it was moved to the BET group which preferred Leylands and AECs. When Bristol chassis became restricted to the nationalised Tilling group, it prolonged the life of almost all its pre-war Bristols by rebuilding and rebodying them. It bought the Dennis Loline – a clone of the Bristol Lodekka – when it came onto the market and was first in the queue for Bristols when they again became generally available in 1966.

With the formation of SELNEC, North Western found itself spread across too many boundaries and the PTE decided the only solution was to take over the company's operations within its area. What was left was not commercially viable and on March 4th 1972, 272 former North Western buses passed to SELNEC and the rest were split between Trent, Crosville and the National Bus Company's North Western coaching unit.

North Western's demise was regretted by staff, passengers and enthusiasts alike. Its last General Manager, Robert Brook, put it nicely when he wrote '... *it took an Act of Parliament to kill it*'.

North Western's home town was Stockport and it occupied the majority of the stands at the south end of Mersey Square. Leyland-bodied PD2 236 is going to New Mills on a 27X, its driver about to climb up and set the number blind. Willowbrook-rebodied Bristol K5G 404's driver is leaning down to start its Gardner 5LW engine, shattering any peace and quiet there was. At the back, a crowd waits to board K5G 462 on the short journey to Bridge Hall Estate. Both Bristols would soon be withdrawn and the PD2 would last only a year longer. *Summer 1964, Photobus*

40

Bristol K5G 463, waiting in Manchester's Chorlton Street bus station to depart on limited stop 52 to Wilmslow and Alderley, is in the 'proper' livery with black edging between red and cream and older style fleet number transfers. The 52 was one of the routes operated 'by arrangement' with Manchester which meant that the corporation did not work it but received an agreed sum for each passenger travelling within its boundary. The horse drawn cart in the background must have been one of the last both in the city and the substantial fleet of carrier Thomas Huskinson. *September 1960, Geoffrey Morant*

Leyland-bodied PD2 464 was a windfall when North Western was short of buses in 1952. A twice-cancelled order for independent operators, North Western bought it 'as seen' complete with non standard indicators, which it modified before 464 entered service, and brown interior trim, which it left. On a busy day at Lower Mosley Street bus station, Manchester, 464 has been hastily summoned from Stockport to help shift the crowds waiting for the X60 to Blackpool. Also waiting in Calder Street at the side of the bus station are a Ribble Leyland Royal Tiger coach and another North Western PD2. *May 1959, John Kaye*

The services from Manchester to Urmston and Flixton were jointly operated by the corporation and North Western. The 5, 11, 12 and 23 started from Piccadilly and the 3 from Cannon Street. Although the latter's roots were in the late 1920s limited stop service from Flixton to Bacup, it always seemed a surprise to find a North Western in Cannon Street and was a reminder that you could find one almost anywhere in the area east of a line from Rochdale though Manchester to Warrington. 1953 Weymann-bodied PD2 550 is seen with Manchester PD2 3442 and PD1 3075. *August 1964, Ron Barton*

Out into Cheshire and Derbyshire, single-deckers were the rule. With a background of the Cheshire Plain towards Stockport on the left of the picture and the foothills of the Peak District on the right, Weymann-bodied Leyland Tiger Cub 699 is in the country lanes between Poynton and Pott Shrigley on North Western's hourly service 8 from Stockport. *Summer 1965, Photobus*

North Western's red, cream and black express livery looked very smart but you would be just as likely to find 1960 Willowbrook-bodied AEC Reliance 804 leaving this stand in Lower Mosley Street bus station on a 32 to Higher Poynton or a 29 to Macclesfield as on a duplicate to Leeds. *1965, Photobus*

The low roof height of North Western's garages dictated its need for low height double-deckers although in the case of the Manchester 91, jointly extended in April 1960 to the new overspill estate at Partington, there was a low bridge between Carrington and Partington. North Western worked it as Manchester had no low height double-deckers at the time. With Bristols still only available to the nationalised bus companies, North Western was quick to order the Dennis Loline, a Bristol Lodekka made under licence. Fifteen with East Lancs bodies arrived in 1960, 812-814 with Gardner 6LX engines and 815-826 with Leyland O.600. New and shiny 822 is seen in Piccadilly bus station. *September 1960, Geoffrey Morant*

Thirty five more Lolines, 872-906, with Gardner engines and Alexander bodies followed in late 1961 and early 1962. Arriving from Altrincham, 903 is on Exchange Street, Stockport. Although they ran right through Manchester and Stockport territory, North Western established the two services between Stockport and Altrincham in the 1920s (71 via Gatley, 80 via Didsbury) and had exclusive rights to them. *October 1969, Geoffrey Morant*

Glossop was North Western's. It had a garage in the town, provided the local services and had a share in limited stop services 6 and 125 to Manchester. With Dennis losing interest in the Loline, in 1963/64 North Western bought 33 low height AEC Renowns with Park Royal bodies and 35 Alexander-bodied Daimler Fleetlines. Renown 125 from the 1964 batch is in Ashton bus station. The destination 'Manchester LMS' appeared on the company's blinds for years. Meaning Lower Mosley Street, it confused unfamiliar travellers who thought LMS referred to one or other of the former railway company's stations at London Road (later Piccadilly), Victoria or Exchange. *April 1969, Geoffrey Morant*

Sixty more Alexander-bodied Daimler Fleetlines followed in 1965 and 1967. New in 1965, 188 and 189 had a complex Compas heating system, the ducts for which reduced the size of a window on both sides of the lower deck. Seen here in Mersey Square, 189 also had a Cummins engine. Very much a standard for buses from the 1980s, in 1965 its use in the United Kingdom was uncommon and it was replaced by the usual Gardner 6LX in 1970. Alongside on the corporation stands is Stockport 59. *April 1969, Roy Marshall*

North Western's last new double-decker, Fleetline 254 of 1967, runs alongside the Hayfield branch line as it approaches Hayfield on the 28 from Manchester, another of the 'by arrangement with Manchester' services. The railway closed in 1970. *Summer 1968, Photobus*

The limited clearance of the bridge under the Bridgewater canal at Dunham Woodhouses on the 'back road' from Altrincham to Lymm required low height vehicles. When the Bristol L5Gs were withdrawn, in 1964 North Western bought ten lightweight Bedford VAL, 130-139, with Strachan bodies, their roofs specially shaped to fit the bridge's arch. In Broadheath, Altrincham, 136 turns from Atlantic Street into Manchester Road en route to Warrington on the peak hour 210. *April 1970, Geoffrey Morant*

Changes in the ownership of Leyland and Bristol in 1965 resulted in Bristol chassis again becoming available on the open market and North Western was first in the queue. Forty 30ft-long Gardner-engined Bristol RE, 270-309, with Marshall of Cambridge bodies joined the fleet in 1968 and were soon a familiar sight in Warrington, Altrincham, Stockport, Ashton, Glossop, Oldham and Rochdale. 279 is in Henry Street, Glossop on a local service. *1971, Photobus*

Thirty 36ft-long Alexander-bodied Gardner-engined Bristol RE, 315-344, arrived in 1969 followed in 1971 by eighteen (345-362) with Leyland engines and Marshall bodies. 330 is arriving in Warrington on the 102 from Urmston via Partington, Warburton and Lymm. *April 1970, Geoffrey Morant*

The final deliveries before the break up were 373-388, sixteen of an order for thirty Leyland-engined RE with Eastern Coachworks bodies. Also on order were twenty five Bristol VR double-deckers with Eastern Coachworks bodies and five Bristol RE coaches. The coaches went to the NBC's North Western coaching unit, SELNEC got the VRs, Crosville and Trent each got five of the REs and the last four were cancelled. This is 382 in the bus park behind the Wellington Road South arches – much later the new Stockport bus station would be built here. *October 1971, Roy Marshall*

Stalybridge, Hyde, Mossley & Dukinfield

The Stalybridge, Hyde, Mossley and Dukinfield Transport and Electricity Board was a 'Joint Board', although the word Joint was not part of its formal title. A Joint Board was a type of statutory body, each established by individual Act of Parliament with the result that even a simple thing like changing its name required a further expensive Act of Parliament. SHMD, as it was known, changed its title from Tramways to Transport in 1936 but the word Electricity remained to the end.

For most of its existence SHMD was firm in its choice of suppliers of chassis and bodies: Thornycroft for chassis until they ceased to be available in 1937 and then Daimler; Northern Counties for bodies. A good, reliable and durable choice. Creditably, most of its general managers were 'home grown' and each produced his share of innovative ideas, such as experimenting with centre-entrance and high capacity buses and buying Atkinsons, including the sole UK Atkinson double-decker.

When SHMD's first 'outside' general manager, Frank Brimelow, arrived from Middlesbrough in 1957 he introduced a new livery, larger and clearer indicators and an advanced open parking area for most of its fleet of about 84. He also bought the ubiquitous Leyland PD2 – SHMD had never before had a Leyland. In 1962 he left to become general manager at Stockport; his successor, James Wood, had been with SHMD since 1926.

SHMD went back to Daimlers with Gardner engines – but even then with a touch of the unusual.

By 1960 there were very few SHMD buses in the dark green, cream and silver roof livery. 1947 Daimler CVD6 23, one of SHMD's first post-war delivery of five with the usual Northern Counties body, is in Chorlton Street bus station along with Manchester CVG6 4452 on limited stop 18 to Stockport. Unlike other limited stop services, the 21 was solely operated by SHMD. When SHMD proposed it back in 1930 Manchester replied that it would never make money and that SHMD was welcome to work it, keep all the revenue – and carry all the costs. *June 1960, John Kaye*

Generally similar 26-35, also delivered in 1947, had Gardner 6LW engines. This is number 30, in the 'Brimelow' livery, parked in Sackville Street by Ashton Station, awaiting a peak hour turn on service 30 to Hyde and Stockport. The bus behind is from the 36-45 batch which, because the Northern Counties, order book was full, had bodies by Brush. These proved troublesome and were replaced with new Northern Counties ones in 1954. *August 1962, Roy Marshall*

Another picture of the older SHMD livery, this time with the green roof. Full order books again affected the 1949 delivery of Daimlers 46-55, which had Daimler engines and East Lancs bodies. 52 is on Merseyway at the Ashton–Hyde–Stockport–Edgeley stop at the back of Stockport's large Co-op with its clock tower and chimney. Unusually without traffic in this picture, busy Merseyway was a linear bridge with the river flowing beneath; road and chimney would vanish with the building of the shopping precinct but much of the Co-op building would remain. *May 1960, John Kaye*

SHMD's buses worked hard for their living, sometimes at the expense of their external appearance, as instanced by the six shades of green and the missing letters from the fleetname on number 66, the last of a batch of six CVD6s new in 1952. The thick centre pillar of the front upper-deck windows carried ducting for the engine air intake which was drawn through arrays of small holes in the ceiling panels of the upper saloon – it was a Northern Counties so-called 'air conditioning' patent. *Photobus, 1967*

The 'standee' Northern Counties body was devised by general manager L G Stockwell and carried 60 passengers – 34 seated, 26 standing. The first (67), on Daimler's underfloor-engined Freeline chassis, was exhibited at the 1952 Commercial Motor Show where it attracted great interest. This picture shows it in the open parking area of the garage towards the end of its life, by which time it had been renumbered 105. The front indicator layout was curious. *August 1968, Roy Marshall*

L G Stockwell's centre entrance idea also appeared in his next double-deckers, one of which was on the unique and much photographed Atkinson chassis. Less photographed were 71-76, Daimler CVG6 with similar bodies. 74 is parked in Hyde bus station, with its prominent clock. *October 1969, Geoffrey Morant*

Stockwell left to join engine maker Gardner and a new manager was appointed from outside. A native of Bury, Frank Brimelow was Deputy General Manager at Middlesbrough. Things changed. Most noticeable was a new colour scheme of mid green with two cream bands. The body specification for 1957 CVG6s 79-84 was quickly changed to a conventional rear platform and a larger, clearer indicator layout. In this picture 81 is in Lower Mosley Street bus station on limited stop 6 to Glossop. Its bonnet was open and appears to have had a broken catch, for 81 arrived and departed thus. Any thought of overheating can be set aside – Gardner engines ran very cool and were extremely durable. *May 1959, John Kaye*

Above left More changes – shocks even – followed. The next new buses were SHMD's first Leylands. Delivered in 1958/59, PD2s 85-92 had standard rear-platform Northern Counties bodies; eight more followed. The lower-deck high level ventilation windows were an option offered by Northern Counties since 1950 after their introduction on Lancashire United Guy Arabs. Number 90 is in Stalybridge bound for Mossley. *August 1968, Roy Marshall*

Left The 1959 vehicle intake also included three Atkinsons with front-entrance Northern Counties bodies, arranged to carry 34 seated and 26 standing. Their fleet numbers were changed from 93-95 to 110-112 in 1961 when Frank Brimelow renumbered SHMD's single-deckers. 112 arrives at Ashton bus station to take up service to Uppermill on the 154, jointly operated with North Western. *April 1969, Roy Marshall*

Above Having given SHMD something of a shake up during his five years in charge, Frank Brimelow was appointed general manager at Stockport. With new 'home grown' general manager James Wood there was a return to SHMD's preferred Daimler CVG6. 7-12, new in 1964, had Northern Counties front-entrance bodies. This is number 9 in Ashton bus station on service 10 with an Ashton Leyland-bodied Leyland PD2 in the background. *April 1969, Geoffrey Morant*

Above left Twenty five Daimler Fleetlines with Gardner 6LX engines and Northern Counties' standard design of body followed, nine in 1965 and sixteen in 1966, numbered 13-37. Number 36 is in North Western territory – High Street East, Glossop – on the joint service from Stalybridge via Hadfield. *Late summer 1969, Photobus*

Left The 1967 single-deckers were Gardner-engined Bristol RE numbered 113-118. They had the re-styled Northern Counties body. Its indicator already set for the return journey, 115 arrives at Ashton bus station with the railway station in the background. *July 1969, Geoffrey Morant*

Above James Wood's final purchases before SELNEC took over were in SHMD's best tradition of mixing novelty and tradition. Short length Fleetlines 38-47 were to a design developed by Walsall Corporation's unconventional general manager, R Edgeley Cox, featuring a short front overhang and a sliding central door and seating 68 instead of the 74 of the longer Fleetline. They also introduced a bright new livery with more cream and a slightly lighter shade of green. *April 1969, Photobus*

Ashton-under-Lyne

Before the war the majority of Ashton's fleet was Crossley and its first post-war deliveries were six of the firm's new DD42 model with Manchester style bodies. Their numbers (1, 8, 10, 12, 21 and 22) filled gaps in the existing fleet but were changed to 55-60 in a renumbering in 1960, by which time some rebuilding work had been done on the side windows. On a bright sunny autumn day, 58 is parked in Sackville Street waiting to take up a duty on the occasional service to the hamlet of Park Bridge, near Bardsley. *October 1962, Roy Marshall*

Ashton's buses got about. They could be seen in Rochdale, Oldham, Manchester, Glossop, Stalybridge, Hyde and Stockport – and beyond, for Ashton was one of the few municipal operators whose Act of Parliament allowed it to operate private hire to anywhere. Although it did not do much itself, it was a willing partner for other municipalities wishing to get around their own restriction. There was a plentiful supply of 'On hire to Ashton-under-Lyne Corporation Passenger Transport' stickers in exchange, of course, for a suitable fee.

Ashton's garage on Mossley Road was as good an example of an early 20th century municipal transport depot as you could find. The fleet stood out from others with its dark blue, red and white livery, unlike any of the other local fleets, as did the peacock blue and primrose that replaced it in 1955. Both were particularly difficult to capture correctly on film because of the varying blue sensitivities of different maker's film emulsions.

Manchester apart, Ashton was also the only local operator to run modern trolleybuses. Although the majority of its buses were Leylands, like its mighty neighbour, Ashton supported local bus builder Crossley – continuing to buy Crossley bodies after experiencing the usual disappointment with the post-war Crossley's HOE7 engine. It also had the largest number of bus bodies (14) by S H Bond Ltd.

For a small undertaking with a fleet of about 50, there was much of interest at Ashton.

Leyland-bodied Leyland PD2 76 was the highest numbered motor bus in the fleet. One of ten new in 1950 numbered 2-7, 9, 23, 25 and 76, they became 1-10 in 1960. A year before that, 76 leaves Rochdale on its 54-minute journey on the joint Rochdale–Oldham–Ashton service. *Summer 1959, Geoffrey Morant*

Very few Ashton vehicles were still in the red, white and blue livery when colour photographs started to become popular. This is one of five Crossley TDD42 trolleybuses new in 1950, with Manchester-style bodies. Number 78 is at the Portland Street, Manchester terminus of the trolleybus services to Ashton and Stalybridge via Ashton Old Road. *Summer 1957, Don Jones*

Another rare shot of the red, white and blue livery. During the war Ashton was allocated sixteen Guy Arabs with Gardner 5LW engines and Massey utility bodies. Nine were rebodied by Crossley in 1950/51; 67 was one. New in 1945, rebodied in late 1950, it re-entered service in January 1951. Behind the Guy is one of four Leyland-bodied Leyland TD5 new in 1939, numbered 17-20. Facing in the other direction and repainted into the newly-introduced peacock blue livery are a Leyland PD1 and Crossley DD42 10, both with Crossley bodies. *Late 1954, Geoffrey Hyde*

Five more Guys were rebodied in 1955 – three by Crossley on Park Royal frames and two by Roe. This is Roe-rebodied number 74. *Summer 1965, Peter Whitworth*

58

New in 1955 were seven Leyland PD2 with Crossley bodies, numbered 11, 24, 29-31, 46, 47 and changed to 11-17 in 1960. By this time Crossley was a member of the ACV Group which directed that Crossley use group member Park Royal's body frames; Ashton's seven were the first examples. The change was not one for the better and they proved to be nothing like as durable as those with Crossley frames. Number 14 in Ashton bus station, opened in 1963, on the former trolleybus service to Denton and Haughton Green jointly operated with Manchester, along with Manchester 3452 on the 219 and an SHMD Fleetline. *April 1969, Geoffrey Morant*

In 1954/55 Ashton chose Bond for new bodies for two wartime Sunbeam trolleybuses and followed this with orders for bodies for four new Guy Arabs and eight new BUT trolleybuses. A well established high quality coachbuilder, Wythenshawe-based Bond was making a determined and successful effort to enter the market for bus bodies. The Guys arrived in May 1956; this is the last of the four, originally numbered 40 and changed to 68 in 1963. They would be the only Guys in the SELNEC fleet. *Geoffrey Morant, April 1969*

The eight new BUT trolleybuses followed in September and October of 1956. At dusk on a wet summer evening Bond-bodied 88 leaves Stalybridge bus station for the 40 minute run through Ashton to Manchester. *Summer 1966, Reg Wilson*

Bond's bodies were finding a ready market when the loss of a senior manager and the union demarcation disputes that had caused Leyland to cease bus bodybuilding, some two years earlier. Bond, too, was forced to give up and returned to its former work. Ashton then turned to Roe, eventually buying 29 bodies on Leyland PD2 chassis, the last five of which had front entrances, and eight on Leyland Atlanteans. One of eight PD2s new in 1962, 27 leaves Lower Mosley Street bus station, Manchester, on service 6 to Glossop. Ribble Atlantean 1687 is waiting to depart on the express service to Skipton. *April 1969, John Kaye*

On service 6, headed for Lower Mosley Street bus station but with its blind already changed for the return journey, Roe-bodied Atlantean 47 pulls away from the Aytoun Street traffic lights in Portland Street, Manchester. The grey building on the extreme right of the picture is 55 Piccadilly, former head office of Manchester Corporation Transport. *1968, Anonymous photographer via David Beilby*

Ashton bought two new single-deckers in 1967 – its first such purchase since 1938. 55 and 56 were Leyland Panther Cubs with East Lancs bodies. 56 is seen in the bus station. An unusual feature was that they had a mixture of coach-type seats with four rows of ordinary bus seats over the rear wheel area. By the time of this photograph Ashton had a new general manager. Peter Bland came from Manchester Corporation and introduced some of that city's ideas including fare boxes for fare collection – 56 is fitted with one in this picture. *August 1968, Roy Marshall*

Peter Bland chose Northern Counties bodies for five Leyland Atlanteans in 1969 and four more which were delivered after SELNEC took over. Fitted for one-man operation, they entered service on the Hurst and Smallshaw circulars using Manchester's Minimax flat-fare system. On its first day in service and not yet fitted with a nearside indicator blind, 61 enters the bus station. *April 1969, Geoffrey Morant*

Oldham

With a fleet of around 230, Oldham was next in size after Manchester, Salford and Bolton but it probably came equal first with Salford in terms of civic pride. Pretty well any Oldhamer one met would be proud of the town's buses. From 1931 the majority of Oldham buses were tough reliable Leylands with quality bodies by Roe. Its crimson lake and white livery, lined out in red for much of the period, was not the easiest to keep clean in a town where cotton mill chimneys dominated the skyline but it managed to do so. In a search for something brighter and more durable, the livery was changed in 1966 to a strange pinkish crimson, called pommard, and a rich cream.

Oldham's tram services had numbers which were retained when converted to bus operation. However, services that were always bus-operated had letters and Oldham folk talked about an 'A-bus' or the 'D-bus'. This intriguing mix continued until the letters were changed to numbers in 1968.

In the mid-sixties the bus fleet's maintenance was hit by shortage of staff, attracted away by the influx of new modern industries which offered better paid jobs. An unnecessarily harsh ministry inspection in 1965 put some 40% of its buses off the road for a short period and local municipalities rallied round to lend vehicles.

Oldham's operating terrain was hard – set more than half way up the western side of the Pennines, with the town centre 700ft above sea level and its outer territory rising to 1000ft, steep gradients were the norm. Even the main road from Manchester to Oldham involved a 540ft climb. Winter ice and snow made it even harder. Before the opening of the M62 motorway, the majority of light and heavy traffic to and from Yorkshire went through the town centre. As if to reassure itself that its choice of supplier was right for this arduous work, from time to time it would buy small batches from other chassis and body makers.

Oldham always went back to Leyland and Roe.

Oldham's first deliveries after the war were fourteen 7ft 6in wide Leyland PD1s with Roe bodies. Post-war austerity restrictions meant that 228-241 did not have the saloon heaters normally standard in Oldham's buses. 231 is in Rochdale Road, High Crompton, bound for Royton on a peak hour run on the normally single-deck F service. Shaw is in the background with Grains Bar, highest point in Oldham's territory, on the skyline behind the bus. *July 1964, Peter Whitworth*

Following from the 7ft 6in Roe-bodied PD1s, fifty 8ft wide ones, 242-291, were delivered in 1947/48. The bodies on the second twenty five did not have the distinctive Roe 'waist rail' below the lower deck windows as on 276 pictured here. Twenty five of Leyland's larger engined PD2 followed and looked much the same apart from their cast aluminium radiator cowls. *1962, Peter Whitworth*

Before the war Oldham had placed orders for 22 Daimler single-deckers. The war put a stop to this but in the immediate post-war rush to get new buses it was not surprising that Oldham turned to Daimler for 25 CVD6 double-deckers, ten with Roe and fifteen with Crossley bodies. Not long before withdrawal, Crossley-bodied 327 of 1949 was photographed at the Greengate, Moston, terminus of the D. The dropped level of the canopy valence above the engine accommodated the saloon heater. *Mid 1966, Peter Whitworth*

Like many of its neighbours, Oldham was persuaded to buy the post-war Crossley. Its first, in 1948, were 7ft 6in wide Roe-bodied single-deckers 292-301. The HOE7 engine was better matched to the lighter weight of a single-deck bus and they gave good service, running high mileages. 295 is at the F-bus terminus at Shore Edge Chapel in Buckstones Road. *1962, Peter Whitworth*

Also in 1948 came ten Crossley DD42 double-deckers with Crossley bodies, 302-311. Two years later, Crossley having developed the improved 'downdraught' version of its HOE7 engine, Oldham bought four more, 366-369, and four more single-deckers, 362-365. They looked much the same as the earlier examples, although power output, fuel consumption and reliability was much better. *1962, Peter Whitworth*

Left Oldham's spacious garage at Wallshaw Place in the town centre opened in 1938. Inside, the notice on the wall exhorted drivers to exercise care, courtesy and consideration. 370 was the first of three Leyland-bodied Leyland PD2s delivered in 1952. Oldham's general manager, Cyril Paige, retired in 1961 and he was succeeded by his deputy, Harry Taylor, who had joined from Liverpool two years before. Fleet number plates instead of transfers were used at Liverpool and Harry Taylor introduced them at Oldham. *June 1967, Peter Whitworth*

This has rightly been described as the best colour picture ever taken of an Oldham bus. Granted 448 is not new but it is in original condition, resplendent with red lining out and shaded fleet number transfers. Oldham bought a total of ninety more Leyland PD2s; fifty four with this style of Roe body. 448 is in Lever Street, Stevenson Square, Manchester, waiting to depart on joint Manchester, North Western and Oldham limited stop service 13. Its 56-minute 14-mile journey would take it through Oldham into Yorkshire, climbing 834 ft to Scouthead and then descending 434ft to Uppermill. *October 1962, Roy Marshall*

The bodies of the other thirty six PD2s were divided between Crossley (5), Northern Counties (6 and 10) and Metro-Cammell (5 and 10). Personal opinion, of course, but they were nothing like as handsome as the Roe. The Park Royal-framed Crossley ones, 408-412 of 1957, proved less durable, only the much-rebuilt 409 surviving to run for SELNEC. 408 is at the Clegg Street terminus of circular service V. By one of those splendid quirks, the trams had operated in both directions showing 4, but when buses took over the anticlockwise circular was lettered V whilst the clockwise service remained the 4. *1966, Peter Whitworth.*

Metro-Cammell's Orion design was durable but, even in Oldham's lined out livery, not one of the most attractive with its differently sized windows. Less so when it had a pinched in front to match with Leyland's front cowl that was designed to fit a 7ft 6in wide bus. Oldham's 1966 pommard livery and replacement front grille did nothing to improve it. 422 in West Street on service 21 (formerly B) from Middleton Junction bound for Fitton Hill. *April 1969, Roy Marshall*

This is 418, one of the 1957 batch of Northern Counties-bodied PD2s, at the Stevenson Square, Manchester, terminus of the main stopping service to Oldham. The 98 ran through the town to the then Yorkshire boundary at Waterhead. There was a bus every five minutes, many more at peak hours, and a journey time of 48 minutes outwards (up the hill) and 46 back down. Manchester provided 13 buses and Oldham 7. *October 1962, Roy Marshall*

Its fleet updated, Oldham needed no more new buses until 1964 when ten handsome front-entrance Leyland PD3s with Roe bodies arrived. 101-110 were Harry Taylor's first purchases and introduced some new features, most noticeable of which was a more comprehensive front indicator display. This is the first of the batch at the New Hey terminus of limited stop service 2 to Manchester. It ran every 20 minutes, Oldham, Manchester and North Western each providing two buses. *1965, GMTS collection*

In 1964/65 six Leyland Tiger Cubs replaced the first of the Crossley SD42s. 111-114 had Marshall bodies and 115/16 had locally built bodies by Pennine Coachcraft, a subsidiary of Oldham-based Seddon. The first of the Marshalls passes under the railway bridge at Mumps on service 22, formerly the D-bus. *April 1969, Roy Marshall*

In October 1965 40% of the fleet was ordered off the road by an over zealous ministry inspector. Some merited the prohibition but others were banned for such trivia as a tear in a seat cushion. Forty six vehicles were hired from local municipalities – Leylands came from Bolton (6), Bury (2), Manchester (10), St Helens (4), Sheffield (5), Stockport (2) and Wigan (4), AECs from Bradford (3) and Rochdale (4) and Daimlers (6) from Salford. In Oldham's garage, Rochdale 227-229, a Bolton and a Bury are in the first row, Manchesters in the second. *December 1965, Peter Whitworth*

Some of those who helped also offered to sell some of their surplus Leyland PD2s. Oldham bought sixteen – four of the Boltons which had been on loan, eight Sheffields and four from Halifax – it being cheaper than repairing some of the PD1s, Daimler CVD6s and Crossleys. All had Leyland bodies. The acquired buses were repainted in crimson and white and numbered 463-478. 474, formerly Bolton 438, is in the garage with 1950 PD2 353 alongside. *January 1966, Peter Whitworth*

Oldham's first Leyland Atlanteans arrived in 1965 – 121-130 with Roe bodies. The plan had been that 121-124 would have East Lancs bodies, a new supplier for Oldham, but a busy East Lancs could not meet the required delivery date. Seventeen more followed in 1966, the first in the pommard and cream colour scheme – 131-135 with East Lancs bodies and 136-147 Roe. Number 140 passes Christ Church graveyard on Oldham Road, Ashton; another few hundred yards would bring it to its terminus in the bus station. *June 1969, Photobus*

A picture which nicely captures the rugged Pennine foothills with their typical stone-built terraced housing and also the changes that were taking place – the tiny Co-op shop has closed. 1967 Marshall-bodied Leyland Panther Cub 118 is at Shore Edge terminus. *July 1967, Peter Whitworth*

No section about Oldham would be complete without a mill with its chimney. This is Coral Mill at the New Hey terminus of limited stop service 2 to Manchester. New in 1967, 150 was one of five with bodies by East Lancs' associate company, Neepsend Coachworks of Sheffield. Built to East Lancs drawings, they were reputedly not as good as the real thing. *July 1967, Peter Whitworth*

Oldham went back to Roe for the 1969 Atlanteans. 178-182 had features to make them suitable for one-man operation, the most noticeable being the lower positioned front indicator boxes which could be set from the lower deck. The 25/26 Holts Estate service was Oldham's first conversion to double-deck one-man operation, some two months later on June 8th. 180 is at the Clegg Street town terminus but is going nowhere, for it has been the subject of vandalism. The fourth upper-deck window is shattered and has a hole in it; the crew are upstairs examining the damage whilst they and the passengers wait for the changeover bus, on its way from the garage close by at Wallshaw Place. *April 1969, Geoffrey Morant*

Hanson of Huddersfield ran a remarkable stage service to Oldham via Marsden, the A62 over Standedge and the top of the Pennines, turning off to come into Oldham via Uppermill, to a terminus on the far side of Union Street in a lonely part of Greaves Street. One bus worked the service; 55 minutes was allowed for the journey in either direction with only a 5 minute break at each end. That took some doing in the heavy traffic of what was the main trunk road before the M62, let alone in ice, snow or fog. North Western ran a competing service 160 via Scouthead. Return tickets were not interchangeable, something that was a frequent source of vehement dispute between passengers and crews. Pictured in Huddersfield's Upperhead Row bus station, 405 was a Willowbrook-bodied AEC Reliance new in March 1967. The trip would likely be an exciting one as there was snow on the hills. *March 1969, Roy Marshall*

The X12 could not carry local passengers in the Manchester or Bradford areas but North Western had a presence and a garage in Oldham and the X12 carried local passengers 'over the top' and offered a quick ride to, say, Grains Bar or Denshaw for a halfpenny more than a local bus. Willowbrook-bodied AEC Reliance 939 of 1963 turns into West Street, Oldham with the mill chimneys of Chadderton in the background. *March 1970, Geoffrey Morant*

Rochdale

Rochdale was unique – the only Lancashire municipal fleet that had no post-war Leylands. It bought AECs and then, with a change of general manager, Gardner-engined Daimlers before another change brought more AECs – the majority having Gardner engines.

Until the fashion for simplified liveries – largely on cost saving grounds – Rochdale's fleet of 150 looked a class above the rest in a magnificent livery of monastral blue and cream, elegantly lined out in black. The post-war buses had Manchester-style indicators and many of the pre-war ones were altered.

Rochdale buses terminated in the town centre in places like The Esplanade, in front of the town hall and surrounded by parks, trees and flowers, South Parade and The Butts. In summer there were flower boxes on top of the bus shelters too. At Mellor Street, about half a mile to the west of the centre, were the department's splendid red brick offices with a modernised spacious garage behind. However, the small amount of dead mileage to and from garage was avoided by the provision of a town centre parking ground for off-service buses. Across Mellor Street was a comprehensively equipped workshop capable of complex work including major rebuilds.

The number of operators that worked into Rochdale on stage services was greater than any of the other towns. Besides the corporation's AECs and Daimlers, there were buses from Manchester, Oldham, Ashton, Bury, Todmorden, North Western, Hebble, Ribble and Scout – and no visit to Rochdale would be complete without walking along Smith Street to see the classy express coaches of Yelloway, again mainly AECs, in their garage and yard in Weir Street.

Rochdale was a very fine bus town.

Rochdale received fourteen wartime Daimlers and was allocated ten more. However, when 21-30 arrived in 1945 they had timber-framed Massey bodies to Massey's pre-war design. Wartime timber being what it was, all ten needed rebuilding, 28/29 comprehensively so, lasting until 1959 – three years longer than the others. 29 is working the 9C, at the time a peak hour cross-town service from Broad Lane on Oldham Road to Bagslate. *June 1957, Michael Eyre*

When it could get what it wanted Rochdale's post-war choice for bodies was Weymann. New in 1948 were eighteen 7ft 6in wide AEC Regent IIIs 31-48. Subsequent buses were 8ft wide and numbered 201 upwards. 201-222 were Regent IIIs, 201-207 with East Lancs bodies and the others with Weymann. 38 and 202 in the town centre bus park in Smith Street. Service 16 went far beyond the town's boundary to Bacup, an eight mile journey. *June 1957, Michael Eyre*

Services which left the town along Bury Road started in Packer Street at the side of the town hall. It was a short, wide road and departing buses made a 180 degree turn, hence the full right hand lock on 1950 Regent III 225 going to Bamford. Behind, 1953 Daimler CVG6 250 is on the shorter run to Greave. *June 1957, Michael Eyre*

The AEC Regal IV was no lightweight. Rochdale had seven in 1951 with East Lancs bodies and eight more in 1953 with bodies by Burlingham. Both batches were unusual in having dual doors – at the front for loading and at the rear for unloading. Originally 301-315, they were changed to 1-15 in 1956 to free up numbers for the new AECs. Very heavy in weight and fuel consumption, four of the Burlinghams were sold to Lancaster in 1957. East Lancs-bodied number 6 is in Packer Street. *October 1962, Roy Marshall*

1951 Regents 233-237 had East Lancs bodies. 233 is in the simplified livery introduced in 1961 – much less attractive but cheaper to apply and in line with the industry fashion of the early sixties. This is Mellor Street with the original brick offices and the modernised and extended garage behind the bus, which is going to take up service on the 17T to Chesham Avenue at the borough boundary on the road to Middleton and Manchester. The T indicated that the journey would go via Tweedale Street, calling at Rochdale Station, instead of Drake Street. *August 1968, Roy Marshall*

General Manager Chaceley Humpidge moved on in 1951 and his successor was Joe Franklin, one of Charles Baroth's Salford team. No surprise, therefore, that the next new double-deckers were Gardner-engined Daimlers. Batches of fifteen arrived in 1953 and 1954 with the usual Weymann bodies. On a hot summer's day, 239 from the first batch and 253, the first of the second batch, are in the town centre bus park in Smith Street. The supervisor's hut was nicely painted in fleet livery. *June 1957, Michael Eyre*

Joe Franklin moved to Blackpool in 1954 and his place was taken by Ronald Cox with Geoffrey Harding as his assistant, also keen on Gardner engines. Both would later have to key posts in Passenger Transport Executives – Ronnie Cox as Director General at Greater Glasgow and Geoff Harding as Director of Operations and Engineering at SELNEC. Contracts were placed for forty AEC Regent V with Gardner 6LW engines and Weymann bodies for delivery in 1956 (268-307) – a big order for a fleet of 150. The Gardner option was not offered for 308-318 in 1957 or 319-322 in 1959. Visually there was no difference between the Gardner and AEC powered buses but there certainly was in the sound they made. This is AEC-engined 317. Note the flower boxes on top of the bus shelters and the Ashton Leyland on service 9 in the background. *June 1957, Michael Eyre*

The Regent Vs still looked smart when repainted in the 'all cream' livery. Gardner-engined 273 and Fleetline 330 are at Littleborough terminus. Rochdale had several services numbered 8. The Littleborough local services to Shore, High Peak, Calderbrook and Hollingworth Lake all showed 8, as did buses working onto these from Rochdale. Limited stop journeys on service 17 to Manchester were also numbered 8. *October 1968, Geoffrey Morant*

No new double-deckers were needed until 1964 and then only five. By this time there was another general manager; Cox moved on in 1962 and his deputy, J P Procter, took over. 323-327 were Daimler Fleetlines with Weymann bodies; seven similar ones, 328-334, followed in 1965. On 324 at the foot of Drake Street in Rochdale centre, the conductor is changing the destination blind for the next journey to Ashton. *July 1969, Roy Marshall*

In much the same way as Oldham and for the same reasons, the indicator display on the last batch of Fleetlines, 335-344, was revised and dropped downwards to make it easier for changing the blinds with one-man operation. The destination was moved to beneath the number and intermediate displays – Manchester staff probably reflected that they had made this alteration back in 1953. 341 is in West Street, Oldham. *April 1969, Roy Marshall*

The replacement of the single-deck fleet was interesting. First came two batches of AEC Reliances – three in 1964 and six in 1966. The next four single-deckers were single-deck Daimler Fleetlines – in the SELNEC area only Bury and Rochdale had them. 30-33 had Willowbrook bodies. In Smith Street in the town centre, 33 has arrived on the cross-town 7/7A from Wardle and is pulling round onto the Healey stand. Behind it Fleetline 328 is taking on a full load for New Hey, having come from Littleborough on cross-town service 3. *July 1969, Roy Marshall*

1969 saw a return to AEC with four rear-engined Swifts, 34-37, their bodies built in Oldham by Pennine; this is 36, again on the 7A. One further single-decker was acquired – a former Fleetline demonstrator but it did not arrive until after SELNEC took over – and ten more AEC Swifts were on order. *July 1969, Roy Marshall*

This picture was taken in April 1970 after SELNEC took over. The Rochdale legal owner and coat of arms have gone but it is a fine vignette of the Rochdale fleet at the end and the lighting of a waning sun with a background of clouds seems appropriate. Left to right in Smith Street bus park are Willowbrook-bodied AEC Reliance 24, Gardner-engined Regent 305, East Lancs-bodied Reliance 23, single-deck Daimler Fleetline 30 and Weymann-bodied double-deck Fleetlines 326 and 333. There is another sign of change – the Bradford Equitable's building was being demolished. *April 1970, Geoffrey Morant*

Rochdale was the boundary of the territories of North Western, coming in from the Oldham direction to the east, and Ribble from the west. Ribble's long 158 service from Blackpool ran via Preston, Blackburn and Edenfield. Scout Motor Services of Preston was a joint operator on the 158 and its maroon, black and cream Leylands worked into Rochdale. Scout 8 (above) and Ribble 1377 (below) are in Packer Street by the town hall. Both are Leyland-bodied Leyland PD2s. *June 1957, Michael Eyre; October 1962, Roy Marshall*

North Western's presence was its one bus share in the joint-with-Rochdale service to Shaw, which terminated in Smith Street. Rochdale's service number was 15; North Western's was 155, altered to 15 in 1965. This is Oldham garage's Marshall-bodied Bristol RE 281A – the 'A' suffix indicated that is was fitted for one-man operation. Behind on the 24 stand for Manchester via Royton is Manchester 3706, one of the city's final batch of Leyland PD2s, recognisable by the heater air intakes at the sides of the destination indicator. *Summer 1969, Photobus*

Hebble's dark red buses worked the 28 stage service into Rochdale from Leeds or Halifax via Ripponden and it was a wild journey over Blackstone Edge if the weather was bad. Its terminus was across the road from that of the 15 and 24. This picture, however, is at the Halifax end of the route, Hebble 189, a Willowbrook-bodied AEC Reliance, having just completed its heady trip over Blackstone Edge. Hebble's bus operations were later sold to Halifax which brought the latter's green, orange and cream buses into Rochdale. *August 1969, Roy Marshall*

To get to or from Todmorden passengers usually had to change from a Rochdale bus to a Todmorden one at Littleborough Summit but on Saturdays limited stop service 20 ran through. Todmorden 37, a Leyland Leopard with East Lancs body, is arriving in Rochdale. It is passing Oldham's Roe-bodied Atlantean 128, waiting at the terminus of the 24 to Manchester via Royton, the former Yelloway service. Behind is Weir Street and Yelloway's office, the roof of its garage is above and to the right of the bus shelter. *July 1969, Roy Marshall*

Yelloway sold its limited stop service to Manchester via Royton to the corporations of Oldham, Rochdale and Manchester in 1944. It became the 24, the terminus remaining outside Yelloway's Weir Street premises. However, no visit to Rochdale would be complete without a look at Yelloway's garage and coach station. A line of Duple and Harrington-bodied AEC Reliances wait in Weir Street. Yelloway was there with an orange and cream livery long before SELNEC. *1970, Photobus*

Bury

Renowned for its black puddings and market, Bury has also produced more than its share of famous people – John Kay invented the flying shuttle which revolutionised weaving, John Peel went to London and founded the modern British police force and then became Prime Minister; more recent sons and daughters of the town include Cherie Blair, wife of another Prime Minister, and famous footballers Gary and Philip Neville.

Bury's fleet of just under 100 buses, mainly Leylands with Weymann bodies, was attractively finished in pale green and cream and their destination blinds included interesting-sounding places like Jericho, Old Duke, Three Arrows, Starling, Stopes, Heap Bridge, Little Lever and Water.

There were some unusual buses, too. In 1947 local politics brought two neat little Guy Wolf 20-seaters for a service to Nangreaves. Years later in 1969 a 21-seat Bedford was bought for the 18 to Topping Fold and 32 to Chesham Road. The twenty five 30ft Leyland PD3s had rear-entrances with platform doors; a sole Guy Wulfrunian proved as troublesome as Wulfrunians elsewhere and was sold after only two years. In 1964 Bury went to Alexander of Falkirk for bodies – the only municipal ones in the Greater Manchester area.

There were two bus garages. The main one on Rochdale Road was easily found, less so the other which was tucked away across the road behind the electricity workshops and stores.

From 1917 to 1991 electric trains ran from Manchester to Bury and provided added transport attraction. It was therefore strange to find that of the thousand or so candidate pictures for this book, there were fewer of Bury buses than any of the other fleets.

Having been allocated five Crossleys in 1946, Bury was then able to get the Leylands it wanted. There were forty three PD1s, fifteen with Roe bodies, thirteen by Northern Counties and fifteen with Bury's preferred choice of Weymann. Northern Counties-bodied 123 has Weymann-bodied 146 behind, both new 1947. Both are in nice condition but 123 would be sold for scrap in 1963 and 146 a year later. *October 1962, Roy Marshall*

New in 1949/50, Weymann-bodied Leyland PD2s 151-175 had air-pressure brakes. This is 172 on Bolton Road near Three Arrows en route to Bolton on the 23T. The T of the 23T was often said to mean 'through' as Bolton's 23 ran only as far as the borough boundary at Breightmet. In fact there was more to it. The 23 service started as part of the inter-town network of the late twenties and ran from Bolton via Bury and Heywood to Rochdale – and that T suffix was originally a Rochdale one, meaning 'via Tweedale Street'. The war caused the service to be split at Heywood and then at Bury. Through working to Rochdale was never restored but that T survived. *1964, Photobus*

The updated four-bay version of the elegantly styled Weymann body looked smart in Bury's livery. Also on the 23T is 180, one of nine Weymann-bodied Leyland PD2s, 178-186, new in 1953. August 1965, *John Kaye*

Of more interest than 178-186 were AEC Regents 176 and 177 which arrived a few months previously. Three Regent chassis are supposed to have been ordered for bodying as fire engines. When the first of these arrived it is said that there was something of a fuss in the council about supporting local industry and that Leylands should be bought. The story continues that the other two chassis were deferred until the kerfuffle had died down and then passed to the transport department which put them in storage until Weymann was ready to body them. The only fact known to the authors is that one of them saw two dusty AEC chassis in store in the garage at the back of the electricity workshops.
September 1969, Roy Marshall

There was a four year gap before the next new buses and, with all those Leylands, the Tiger Cub chassis might well have been expected to be the choice for 1957 single-deckers 81-86. Instead the order went to AEC for Reliances with Weymann bodies to the BET group's standard design. The main garage was not over large and during the day some buses would be parked on spare cleared ground at its side. *1968, Photobus*

Perhaps the 'stars' of Bury's fleet were the twenty five rear-entrance Weymann-bodied Leyland PD3s bought by new general manager Frank Thorp. 201-225, new in 1958/59, looked particularly smart with their cream front domes and were different in having platform doors – unusual for local town services. There is added interest in the background of this picture of 224 leaving Rochdale centre on the 21T. The name and logo of the cinema are the right colours and shape for an AEC badge – very appropriate in Rochdale. It was the standard logo of the Associated British Cinemas group which was started in 1927, its logo inspired, maybe, by someone coming too close to the front of a London bus. *July 1960, Geoffrey Morant*

In line with the trends of the sixties, Bury's livery was simplified although nothing like so much as at Manchester and Rochdale. The arrangement of the cream on the front and rear domes was altered to something more conventional, the dark green mudguards were changed to the same colour as the rest of the body and the coat of arms moved to the front side panels of the upper deck. More subtly, the green was changed to a slightly brighter shade. 218 leans over as it turns round the apex of Kay Gardens, around which many of Bury's services terminated. *June 1969, Reg Wilson*

A fine study of two Bury Leylands parked on the spare ground outside the Rochdale Road garage. Both have Weymann bodies. 183 was a PD2, one of nine new in 1953 with Weymann's particularly elegantly-styled four-bay body. The previous batches of PD2s had air pressure brakes but 178-186 reverted to vacuum. There was a gap of five years before the next new double-deckers arrived – 30ft-long Leyland PD3s 201-225. Both buses have the coat of arms at the front of the upper deck sides but still have the smart dark green mudguards. *August 1968, Roy Marshall*

Leyland Atlanteans arrived in 1963. 102-116 had Metro-Cammell bodies to the striking design produced by Liverpool Corporation as a more acceptable alternative to Metro-Cammell's own bland offering and it was surprising that only two other operators – Bury and Bolton –bought it. One replaced little used Wulfrunian 101, new in December 1960. Washed by an April shower, brand new 110 loads on the 37 Walmersley – Bury – Whitefield service; behind, Bolton 408 is on the 23T. *April 1963, Roy Marshall*

New in 1964, 117-131 were Daimler Fleetlines with Alexander bodies, the only municipal examples in the Manchester area. Service 52, a Bolton series number, was an alternative way to Bolton to the more direct 23T and went via Radcliffe, Little Lever and Farnworth. Eighteen month-old 118 is in Howell Croft South bus station, Bolton. *August 1965, John Kaye*

Alexander also supplied the 43-seat bodies for 1964 AEC Reliance single-deckers 87 and 88. The service to Nangreaves, a tiny hamlet perched on the hill above Walmersley (Ordnance Survey maps call it Mount Pleasant), started after a successful 'elect me and I'll get you a bus service' promise by a candidate in the council elections. Because of turning problems, service 49 had to be worked by small buses – hence the two little Guys in 1948. In 1955 space was found for a proper reversing bay, enabling use of 30ft buses. *September 1969, Roy Marshall*

Without the usual peaks and wrap around windscreen, this East Lancs body's styling was an evolution from bodies on front-engine chassis. It was supplied to Warrington, Coventry, Sheffield and Bury, which took six Fleetlines in 1965. New general manager Norman Kay also introduced a revised indicator layout. He went on to senior posts at SELNEC before becoming Director General of the South Yorkshire PTE. 137 loads in Kay Gardens for Rochdale. *May 1969, Geoffrey Morant*

Weight restrictions on the bridge over the railway at Trinity Street, Bolton caused problems with the 23T. Bolton services which used the bridge were diverted but the timings on the 23T made this impractical. Bolton still had plenty of relatively new 27ft long double-deckers but Bury's dated from 1953 and it decided to buy four new Leyland PD2s with East Lancs front-entrance bodies. New in 1967, 187-190's fleet numbers followed on from the 1953 PD2s; this is 187. *August 1968, Roy Marshall*

Along with the PD2s there were three single-deck Daimler Fleetlines, 89-91 with East Lancs bodies. *April 1969, Roy Marshall*

The 1968 batch of Fleetlines, 138-143, had the more typical East Lancs body. Most of Bury's services stopped around the triangular Kay Gardens, which were always nicely tended. Complete with topiary, they were ablaze with flowers in the summer and sitting on one of the park benches whilst waiting for a bus was very relaxing. *May 1969, Geoffrey Morant*

92-97 were single-deck Daimler Fleetlines with East Lancs dual-door bodies seating 41 with space for 19 standing. New in 1969 they were finished in a bright new livery which used a very pale cream instead of the previous primrose. Three similar vehicles of 1967 were in the old livery. The building on the right is the famous Bury Market Hall which was open every day. On market days – Wednesday, Friday and Saturday – there would also be dozens of outside stalls. A delicacy to enjoy as you walked round the market was a Bury black pudding eaten hot from a paper bag. *May 1969, Geoffrey Morant*

Fleet numbering restarted at 1 in 1969 with three East Lancs-bodied Leyland Atlanteans in the new livery. The Atlanteans seem to have been something of a tactical purchase as the next double-deck order, not delivered until SELNEC took over, was for seven more Fleetlines which would have been numbered 4-10. This is the last of the three Leylands in Howell Croft South, Bolton; behind is Lancashire United Alexander-bodied Bristol RE 304. *Summer 1969, Photobus*

There were echoes of the Guy Wolf when a Bedford J2 with a Willowbrook 21-seat body was bought to start two short services to Chesham Road, off Walmersley Road and Topping Fold, off Rochdale Old Road. It took the number of the first of the 1957 Reliances to be withdrawn, 81, and was the last new Bury Corporation bus. The flowers in Kay Gardens are in bloom, surrounding the monument to John Kay, inventor of the flying shuttle. *September 1969, Roy Marshall*

Ramsbottom

Bringing Ramsbottom Urban District Council's 13-vehicle bus fleet into SELNEC seemed to make little sense. Ramsbottom was closer to Rawtenstall than to Bury and for some years had shared a general manager with the Rawtenstall and neighbouring Haslingden undertakings as a step towards merging the three fleets. Older or surplus buses were already swapped between the three and Rawtenstall and Haslingden went on to form the Rossendale Joint Omnibus Committee.

Small it was but its traditional dark red and cream bus fleet was very up to date. When SELNEC took over, Ramsbottom's oldest vehicle was less than nine years old and half the fleet was under three years. In its recent past it had scored the odd 'first'. In 1950, for example, it became the first in the country to take delivery of and operate the then new underfloor-engined Leyland Royal Tiger bus; in 1947 it had been one of the first to operate the Leyland PD2, and the year before was the first to operate the Leyland PS1. On order but not delivered until SELNEC took over was the last forward-engined Leyland Titan PD built.

There was, presumably, some reason somewhere for Ramsbottom's becoming part of SELNEC.

Ramsbottom's service into Bury terminated outside Bury's art gallery in Moss Street, across the road from Kay Gardens. This is 1952 Leyland Royal Tiger 30 in immaculate condition in 1956. The highest numbered bus in the fleet, its sparkling paintwork stands out against the smoke blackened exterior of the art gallery – the latter would be equally bright after it was cleaned in the 1960s. Ribble had dozens of similar buses but Ramsbottom's was the only example of Leyland's post-war single-deck bus body in the Manchester-area municipal fleets. *1956, Phil Tatt*

Having renewed its fleet with seven Leyland PD2s, four PS1s and four Royal Tigers, no more new buses were needed until the 1960s. From 1961 one or two new Leylands were bought each year, all with East Lancs bodies. Fleet numbering restarted at 1 with this 1961 PD2 pictured in Ramsbottom on the Edenfield – Ramsbottom – Bury service. Stubbins, shown on the bus's destination blind, was the location of Ramsbottom's garage. *June 1966, Geoffrey Morant*

New in 1963, number 3 was a PD2A, the A indicating the so-called St Helens style of front cowl. It was Ramsbottom's first front-entrance double-decker and its final PD2 – future purchases were 30ft long PD3s. Road works affect its route as it arrives in Rawtenstall, passing the local Co-op. Although both were joint with Bury and Rawtenstall, the service via Ramsbottom was worked solely by the Urban District Council's buses whilst that via Walmersley to Rawtenstall and Water was operated by Bury and Rawtenstall. *March 1968, Roy Marshall*

Ramsbottom's service list of Bury–Ramsbottom–Edenfield, Bury–Ramsbottom–Edenfield–Rawtenstall and the Ramsbottom–Shuttleworth local, expanded in 1968 with a short feeder to Holcombe village from the main route at Holcombe Brook. This needed a small bus and a 1963 Weymann-bodied Albion Nimbus was acquired from Warrington Corporation which had bought it in 1966 from Halifax. Numbered 12 by Ramsbottom, it is seen at its Holcombe Brook terminus with a couple of passengers. The warning siren on the pole is part of a network of that was still in place across the country. *March 1968, Roy Marshall*

The arrival of the new PD2s made the three Roe-bodied Royal Tigers surplus. As mentioned in the chapter heading, Haslingden, Rawtenstall and Ramsbottom shared a general manager and had plans to merge their operations. With several years of life left in them, two of the Royal Tigers passed to Haslingden and the other to Rawtenstall. This is Haslingden 15, formerly Ramsbottom 27, in Haslingden. *August 1963, Roy Marshall*

For its last six PD3s, Ramsbottom specified the traditional radiator cowl. Numbers 6 and 7 arrived in mid-1967, 8/9 in late 1967 and number 10 in early 1969. Bus 11, the last Leyland PD Titan to be produced, was delivered to SELNEC. It was identical to number 9, photographed here in Manchester Road in Bury centre. There was a regular flow of Ribble buses through Bury on express services but it had only one local service – the 255 to Edgworth, worked here by Marshall-bodied Leyland Leopard 208. *May 1969, Geoffrey Morant*

Bolton

The first sixty seven of the Crossleys, delivered in 1946/47, had bodies by Cravens of Sheffield. Very angular and upright, almost like a wartime utility, the bodies proved durable. 259 is seen in Howell Croft South Bus Station alongside SLT trolleybus 68. The ten year-old bus appears in fine condition but the trolleybus is looking somewhat neglected. The other eight Crossleys had Manchester-style Crossley bodies. *February 1956, Jack Batty*

With some 280 buses, Bolton had the largest fleet after the two cities in this book and from 1924 had been a firm Leyland user. From 1939 to 1959 its general manager was Arthur Jackson and the undertaking was efficiently run with a reliable fleet including 100 PD2s with Leyland bodies. The 75 Crossleys taken into stock after the war for the final stage of the tram replacement were allocated by the ministry – Bolton had applied for Leylands and was not best pleased to be told it had to have Crossleys. Having got them, it made sure that they gave good service and ran a full life span. The main fleet of post-war Leylands had air brakes – very much the norm from the late 1960s but extremely unusual in the United Kingdom in the 1940s and 1950s when vacuum brakes were the rule and Bolton's air-braked PD1s were unique.

It was something of a surprise when Daimlers joined the fleet in 1957 but greater changes were to come when Ralph Bennett took over as general manager on 1st January 1960. It is probably no exaggeration that at Bolton and his succeeding post at Manchester, Ralph Bennett did more to change the image of the British bus for the better than anyone else. New designs, new liveries, innovative services, fares and methods of fare collection – fresh ideas swept through Bolton and Manchester like a hurricane. Bolton's bus fleet was suddenly the focus of attention. Ralph Bennett was not part of SELNEC – from Manchester he moved to London Transport, effectively as chief executive. Sadly the post proved to be a poisoned chalice, beset with political interference and entrenched 'not invented here' attitudes.

All this change would not have happened, however, if Bolton's transport committee had not taken the brave step of appointing him in 1959. Much credit to them.

Rather like Salford, Bolton then placed orders which would eliminate much of the pre-war stock. 100 Leyland air-braked PD2 with Leyland bodies, 351-450, were delivered in 1948 and 1949, the second fifty having a revised indicator layout. The town hall is the background to this picture of 441 at the town terminus of the services to Townley's, Bolton's infirmary and general hospital. Behind is one of fifteen Leyland PD1s with Crossley bodywork. *June 1957, Michael Eyre*

With over 200 of its 280-strong fleet renewed, Bolton needed no new buses until 1955 when fifteen Metro-Cammell-bodied Leyland PD2 arrived. The latter started a new numbering series at 51. 56 is working the Horwich service, which started on the bridge over the railway station in Trinity Street. The '8' on 56's cab door reminded the driver of the bus's width. *1955, Phil Tatt*

Identical twins – almost. Along with the fifteen PD2s of 1955 there was a single Royal Tiger bus. East Lancs built relatively few single-deck bodies and number 9 had one of them. A similar Royal Tiger, 10, followed in 1956 and its body was unique. It was the only single-deck bus body built by Bond and its designer clearly had a good look at number 9. The two are parked in Carlton Street outside the works and garage, off Bradshawgate in the town centre. *June and May 1969, Roy Marshall*

Short of buses, late in 1955 Bolton accepted the offer of the Leyland PD2 demonstrator of S H Bond Ltd, which was making a determined effort to break into the market. Number 66's vacuum brakes made it 'odd man out' in the fleet. Bolton then bought ten more Bond bodies, including the single-decker in the previous picture. Former demonstrator 66 is in Moor Lane bus station in the 1962 Bennett livery; behind is Ribble Tiger Cub 1018 with a Burlingham Seagull body. *March 1968, Roy Marshall*

The choice of body supplier for the 1957 vehicles was one that would continue for much of the department's existence – a roughly 50/50 split between Metro-Cammell and East Lancs. Daimler's CVG6 with pre-selector gearbox was the surprising choice for the chassis – they were Bolton's first ever Daimlers. 85-94 had East Lancs bodies with platform doors for the joint Ribble service to Chorley and Southport, and 95-105 had Metro-Cammell bodies. 103 is in Howell Croft South bus station with PD2 391 and SLT Sunbeam 69. *1958, Jack Batty*

The 1958 intake was of ten Leylands with East Lancs bodies and seven Daimlers with Metro-Cammell, all 30ft long. With Ribble, LUT and corporation buses on the stands in the background, Leyland PD3 113 leaves Moor Lane bus station for Harwood, its paintwork looking tired. *August 1967, Roy Marshall*

Not all of Bolton's services were suitable for 30ft long buses and the next order, was for five rear-entrance 27ft long PD2s and five front-entrance 30ft PD3s. This mix of lengths continued in the following order, which went to Daimler and Leyland. Delivered in 1960 143-150 were 30ft East Lancs-bodied Daimler CVG6-30. 146 is on the 46 service to Hall i'th Wood; now a museum, the 17th century hall was where in 1779 Samuel Crompton invented the Spinning Mule which mechanised the spinning of cotton yarn leading to a massive increase in cotton production in Lancashire. *May 1969, Roy Marshall*

Leyland's delivery times had become long and PD2s 133-142 did not arrive until 1961, by which time Ralph Bennett was in charge. Influenced, it is said, by Ribble's PD3s he altered the design of 133-142's Metro-Cammell bodies to have full fronts. In this picture 135 is ready for a lonely trip up onto the moors to the village of Belmont. The black and yellow plate lettered 'C' in 135's cab window indicated the garage to which the bus was allocated – A for Shiffnall Street off Bradshawgate (Carlton Street overhaul works was on the same site), B for Bridgeman Street and C for Crook Street, all very close to the town centre. *March 1968, Roy Marshall*

No sign of the gritters as the driver of snow covered 1961 East Lancs PD3 156 carefully negotiates the junction of Manchester Road and the new A666 Saint Peter's Way by-pass near Moses Gate, Farnworth. *Winter 1967, Photobus*

The six Metro-Cammell-bodied AEC Regents, 162-167, that completed the 1961 deliveries were a surprise to observers. The short-lived livery of a much lighter red and one wide cream band was modelled on that of Plymouth, where Ralph Bennett had been deputy general manager before moving to Great Yarmouth and then Bolton. *October 1962, Roy Marshall*

Leyland PD3s 168-184 delivered in 1962 and 1963 were Bolton's final front-engined buses and featured full fronts, semi-automatic gearboxes and a new livery. There was the usual East Lancs (9) and Metro-Cammell (8) split for the bodies. The front windscreen was shaped to match the 'St Helens' engine cowl, giving an unusual appearance but affording the driver a better view of the kerb. Six months-old East Lancs bodied 170 leaves Moor Lane for Harwood. There is a fine selection of cars and motorcycles in the adjacent car park, which is not even half full. *September 1962, Roy Marshall*

Jointly with East Lancs, Ralph Bennett produced a stylish new rear-engined body which appeared on Atlanteans 185-192 and 200-218. Translucent panels in the upper-deck roof were a notable feature. The revised indicator display was another Bennett idea with large, easy to see numbers, a white on red blind in the upper box for the outer terminal and white on black in the lower box for the town one. The red had to be changed to green after the police pointed out that showing a red light on the front of the bus at night was illegal. Brand new 185, along with LUT Guy Arab 112, is seen on service 8 in Salford's Victoria bus station. Manchester was shown as the destination on all the inter-town services into Salford – indeed not even Salford's buses could show 'SALFORD' in their indicators. *April 1963, Peter Roberts*

Bolton also bought some Liverpool-style Metro-Cammell-bodied Leyland Atlanteans. 193-199 entered service in July and August 1963. Comparison with the picture of 185 above shows that some of Liverpool's design features were taken into the East Lancs body. *May 1969, Roy Marshall*

Single-decker design also received Ralph Bennett's attention and the result appeared in 1964. First to enter service, on 1st March, were 30ft long Leyland Leopards, 16/17, with stylish East Lancs bodies. Two similar 36ft ones, 14/15, followed a month later. Number 16 is in Great Moor Street bus station. *May 1969, Roy Marshall*

On 1965 Atlanteans 219-226 many details of the Liverpool-style Metro-Cammell body were altered to resemble the East Lancs design, including filling in the sides of the gap above the engine cowl, revising the arrangement of colours and trim on the lower deck and changes to the rear dome. They were Bolton's last Metro-Cammell bodies. Bolton 223 and LUT Guy Arab 234 are in Moor Lane bus station on services that had replaced the SLT trolleybuses in 1958. *May 1969, Roy Marshall*

This nearside shot of East Lancs-bodied Leyland Atlantean 208 shows some of the features copied from the Liverpool design, notably the angle to the side front windows on each deck, and some of the alterations such as the shape of the wheel arches and the panelled in rear "bustle".
May 1969, Roy Marshall

Ralph Bennett moved to Manchester in April 1965 and his deputy Jim Batty took over. 227-286, delivered in 1965/6/7/8, had a wrap around windscreen to reduce the build up of dirt caused by vortices in the air flow round the front of the body. 262 and 259 are seen in Howell Croft South bus station shortly before it closed; the Octagon Theatre was built on the site. *1968, Photobus*

East Lancs-bodied Atlanteans 287-301 were to a striking new design with large windows and sloping pillars. Equipped for one-man operation, they had dual doors to speed passenger flow. Four, including this one, arrived the month before SELNEC took over; the others were delivered to SELNEC in Bolton livery. Significantly, the next order, delivered to SELNEC in orange, reverted to the previous body style. Even the sunshine looks cold in this picture of 300, its lower panels covered with road salt and dirt after a wintry trip to Harwood. *March 1970, Roy Marshall*

Ribble had a significant presence in Bolton. It had a garage with an allocation of between 40 and 50 and, in addition to express services, had a network of stage routes – locally to Dimple and Edgworth, further afield through Chorley to the seaside at Southport (all joint with Bolton) and to Blackburn, Darwen, Burnley, Preston and Morecambe. Burlingham-bodied Leyland PD3 1554 loads for the stopping service to Morecambe. Bolton 133 waits to pull onto the stand for the 122 to Chorley and Southport, the round trip taking four and a half hours. *Summer 1969, Photobus*

Near Holcombe Brook on a bright sunny day, Ribble Atlantean 1651 is inbound on the 236 from Burnley through Rawtenstall, Ramsbottom, Holcombe Brook, Hawkshaw and Bradshaw to Bolton. The bus was one of Ribble's first batch of Atlanteans, 1606-1655, new in 1959/60. *June 1966, Geoffrey Morant*

Based at Howe Bridge, Atherton, Lancashire United Transport ('LUT') was privately owned and not associated with any of the big groups. It was therefore free of the constraints of such things as group purchasing decisions.

LUT had a well-defined operating territory, bounded approximately by a line from Warrington through Wigan, Bolton, Farnworth, Swinton, Eccles back to Warrington, apart from within Leigh's and the other municipalities' boundaries. Like North Western, in 1928 it became a full member of the inter-town limited stop network and had joint operating agreements with all the relevant operators, that with Manchester giving it access to the massive Trafford Park industrial estate. Much of LUT's own area was industrial with cotton mills, coal mines and other factories providing a rich source of traffic.

Managed from 1910 to 1955 by the redoubtable E H (Ned) Edwardes, up to 1948 LUT was a dedicated Leyland user. The occasional batches of Dennises were a link back to 1920 when LUT had been a Dennis agent. During the war the fleet expanded to in order to transport workers to the Royal Ordnance factory at Risley and the United States Air Force base at Burtonwood, bringing fifty seven Guys and four Daimlers into the fleet. The Guys introduced LUT to the economies and reliability of Gardner engines and Northern Counties steel-framed bodies, and from 1948 until the Arab ceased to be available the Guy, Gardner and Northern Counties combination was the norm for LUT's 350-strong fleet – with small numbers of Leylands and Daimlers and, of course, a few more Dennises.

Many of LUT's services were joint with the Passenger Transport Executive and, like North Western, too much of its territory became part of the County of Greater Manchester when it was formed in 1974. In 1976 Lancashire United Transport was bought by the Greater Manchester PTE, which SELNEC PTE had become in 1974. Through no fault of its own, LUT followed North Western into the sea of orange.

LUT's subsidiary, South Lancashire Transport, operated trolleybuses and several of its long lived fleet of Roe-bodied Guys new on the day the system opened in 1930 were still in use, albeit somewhat rebuilt, when the system closed in 1958. A remarkable achievement.

A few of the wartime Guys were later fitted with new bodies but most were rebuilt retaining their original austere shape. New in 1944, Strachans-bodied 317 was the last of the latter to be withdrawn. Here it is at Atherton on its last day in service.
7th July 1963, Peter Roberts

Above left LUT's first post-war double-deckers were Leyland PD1s – twelve in 1946 and ten in 1948. This is 362, new in 1948, in the garage at Swinton. LUT had large garages at Howe Bridge, Atherton, across the road from the offices and works, Platt Bridge, Hindley and Partington Lane, Swinton, the latter being inside Salford's operating area, and a small one in Liverpool. *July 1963, Peter Roberts*

Above right The double-deck Dennis Lance was an uncommon model and LUT's were the only ones in the north west. Nine were new in 1947 and ten more followed in 1948, all with Gardner engines and Weymann lowbridge bodies. When new they and the PD1s were finished in a livery of red with two white bands and a grey roof; on repaint they received the later livery of red with a single cream band. 419 is in the twilight of its years in Swinton garage. *July 1963, Peter Roberts*

LUT shared the X60 Manchester to Blackpool express with North Western and Ribble. In 1948 the latter's new 'White Lady' double-deck coaches prompted LUT to provide something rather better than a PD1 with bus seats. The result was a Guy Arab with 6LW engine and a smart Northern Counties body which had extra windows, styled pillars and a bright cheerful interior with high-backed seats upholstered in patterned moquette. 385-394 entered service in 1949, 425-436 in 1950. Thirty one more followed and they appeared on all of LUT's major services. 436 was specially finished for the Northern Counties stand at the 1950 Commercial Motor Show with the extra feature of glass roof corner panels. *September 1950, Northern Counties via Roy Marshall*

LUT tended to buy its single-deck bodies from Roe but it was unusual for that firm to build coach bodies. It provided ten of these Guy Arabs in 1951. Originally finished in black and red – more or less a copy of Midland Red's coach livery – they were repainted cream and red as 444 is here in Lower Mosley Street bus station. It was withdrawn in 1964. *Summer 1960, Peter Roberts*

Based in Sandbach, Cheshire, Foden built very few double-deckers. Also being in Cheshire, it was appropriate that Chester and nearby Warrington Corporations bought some; that LUT took five was somehow unsurprising. Numbered 447-451, they had Gardner 6LW engines and the same well-equipped Northern Counties body as the Guys. Foden's design of engine cowl was particularly neat and the overall result very attractive. 448 is outside the garage at Howe Bridge. *July 1964, Reg Wilson*

Unable to buy Bristols, North Western's Chief Engineer, Stuart Driver, persuaded Walton-le-Dale, Preston truck builder Atkinson to produce a similarly rugged Gardner-engined chassis. North Western having developed, run and proved prototypes, BET group headquarters rejected Stuart Driver's plan to buy 100 whereupon he quit on the spot. Atkinson persevered and found a good customer at LUT which bought forty over the years 1952 to 1955. Nineteen had Roe bodies with the same high-backed seats as the double-deckers. On Warrington Road, the A573, near the junction of Cemetery Road between Ince and Platt Bridge, 524 is working a short to Tamar on the Leigh–Wigan service. *Summer 1969, Photobus*

When Ned Edwardes retired in 1955 LUT recruited Manchester's Chief Engineer, Cyril Oakham, as general manager and he imported some Manchester features, the most noticeable being the indicator layout. LUT was an early adopter of the 30ft long double-decker and a 30ft Guy Arab with Northern Counties body is probably the most typical LUT bus of the late 1950s and 1960s. 616 was one of thirty new in 1958. In this picture it is in Swinton garage having a new driver's seat fitted. *1971, Photobus*

Presumably hoping that LUT might follow Manchester's policy of a half Leyland, half Daimler fleet, Leyland's sales team must have been pleased by an order for fourteen PD3s, delivered in 1958 and numbered 644-657. The steering wheels of LUT double-deckers were coloured to indicate the height of the bus to the driver – red for high vehicles, black for low height and white for rear-engined. 644 is near Howe Bridge with a full load on the former trolleybus service from Bolton. *1960, Photobus*

After the PD3s, fleet numbering restarted at 1 in 1959 with five AEC Reliances with Burlingham semi-coach bodies, modelled on Duple Donington coaches bought the previous year. LUT had only a few true luxury coaches and most of its coaching work was with semi coaches of this type, painted in reversed livery when new. Repainted in bus livery as newer vehicles arrived, they were still just as likely to appear on long distance express work. Number 5 is in Moor Lane car park, Bolton, ready for an evening tour round the Cheshire lanes. *July 1968, Photobus*

Before Salford and Manchester, LUT had been persuaded to try a non-preselector version of the Daimler – in this case with a David Brown synchromesh gearbox. It bought ten CSG6 in 1959 with the usual Northern Counties bodies. Number 17, the last of the batch, speeds round the Crescent, Salford, on the X60 to Blackpool – nice enough but not quite the same comfort as one of those luxurious Guys. *June 1970, Howard Piltz*

It was somehow inevitable that LUT would buy a few Dennis Lolines – two in 1959 and four more in 1960, all with Northern Counties bodies. The front panel was not deep enough for the full Manchester indicator layout and the intermediate blind was used for destination. They had Gardner engines – just as well as the services on which they were used served Gardner's works. The 14 and 20 ran from Farnworth via Swinton to Patricroft where there was a low railway bridge, the 20 going on to Cadishead and Glazebrook. Loline 7 of 1959 has 6 minutes left of its 36 minute journey from Patricroft as it loads in Farnworth en route to the 14's local terminus at New Bury. *Summer 1969, Photobus*

The X85 was an infrequent subsidised rail replacement service introduced when Glazebury Station closed, providing a link from Wigan through Culcheth to Irlam. Although it operated as a limited stop in parts, the 'X' was window dressing – the number was not in the express series but simply the next vacant after 84 in LUT's bus series. 1961 Guy Arab 76 heads back for Hindley garage on a sunny winter's day. *1970, Photobus*

For rear-engined double-deckers LUT chose Daimler's Gardner-engined Fleetline and Northern Counties bodywork. 97-102 arrived in 1962, followed by a further six in 1962/63. They promptly appeared on the limited stop service 8 from Bolton to Manchester. Operators would often put new vehicles on the inter-town services as if to show off their new buses. 140 is leaving Bolton for Salford. *June 1966, Geoffrey Morant*

Cyril Oakham resigned in 1964 after a disagreement with his fellow directors and Robert Bailey, traffic manager of Potteries Motor Traction, was appointed in his place. With nothing available from Guy or Atkinson, Leyland was the choice for single-deckers 196-217, new in 1965/66. The mix of types indicated things were changing. They included 30ft Leopards with Plaxton coach bodies, 36ft Leopards with Marshall bus bodies, 30ft Tiger Cubs with Willowbrook bus bodies and a solitary Northern Counties dual-door Tiger Cub. Three more Tiger Cubs, 242-244, this time with Marshall dual-door bus bodies, followed in 1968. 244 is outside LUT's office at Spinning Jenny Street bus station, Leigh. *September 1972, Geoffrey Morant*

Guy and Daimler were swallowed up into the Leyland Motor Corporation which swiftly ended production of the Guy Arab. LUT's final batch – twenty six of them – arrived in 1967. Although it had been buying 30ft-long Guy Arabs since 1956, motivated by fuel economy and helped by the flat terrain of its operating area, LUT chose not to adopt Gardner's powerful 6LX engine and stayed with the 6LW for all but one (number 27). Arabs 265-290 had front entrances – as had all LUT's Guy Arabs since 1963. 280 leaves Leigh bus station on the 26 limited stop to Manchester. *August 1968, Roy Marshall*

The pace of changed quickened – with rear-engined Bristol RE, AEC Swift and Seddon RU chassis, the mid-engined Bristol LH and bodies from Plaxton and Alexander as well as Northern Counties but no new double-deckers from 1967 to 1971. In 1968/69 three AEC Swifts, 291-293, were followed by twenty Gardner-engined Bristol RE. They were LUT's first new AECs since 1925 and Bristols since 1927. With similar Alexander bodies, both types looked much the same. Bristol 310 is on private hire to Southport with a Bolton Atlantean behind. Easter holiday weekends were very busy and anything would do. *April 1969, Roy Marshall*

In a new red and grey livery came twenty Bristol LH with Leyland engines and Northern Counties high-capacity dual-door bodies, carrying 39 seated and 16 standing. The LH was a lighter duty chassis than the RE but 318-337 were used on normal services. Bound for Tamar, 322 loads in Wigan bus station with the Fish Market in the background. *June 1971, Roy Marshall*

1970 also saw the arrival of twenty Seddon RU, 338-357 – not quite so surprising as it may seem as they had Gardner 6HLX engines. Plaxton supplied the bodies, again with dual-entrance and high capacity – 40 seated, 19 standing. Thirty more, 364-393, followed in 1971. Here is 353 of 1970 in Spinning Jenny Street bus station on the former trolleybus service to Farnworth alongside a Leigh AEC Renown on the similar service to Bolton. *September 1970, Roy Marshall*

The Daimler Fleetline remained the choice for double-deckers although there was a break from 1965, when five were bought, to 1971, when an equally modest six arrived. The 1972 batch of ten had a mixture of dual- and single-door bodies; ten dual-door ones in 1974 were LUT's last new double-deckers before sale to the PTE. All had Northern Counties bodies, the 1972 and 1974 buses having this attractive arrangement of the new colours. 403, the last of the 1972 delivery, is in Victoria bus station, Salford, on the 8 service. *June 1975, Roy Marshall*

South Lancashire Transport

South Lancashire Transport ('SLT') was owned by Lancashire United. Gone years before SELNEC it was probably the most unique feature of the area's transport.

SLT operated trams and then trolleybuses from the same depots as its parent – Atherton, Swinton and Hindley – on long interurban services from Leigh to Bolton via Atherton, Leigh to Mosley Common Colliery via Atherton, Atherton to Farnworth via Worsley and Swinton, and Atherton to St Helens via Hindley.

The services to Bolton and St Helens were joint with those two corporations but Bolton's four trolleybuses were painted, lettered and numbered as SLT vehicles and operated from Atherton with SLT crews. On the long Farnworth service there was a time break at Swinton and, although there was no change in vehicle, passengers had to rebook. This same rebooking applied at the Bolton boundary; there were no through fares and crews carried an SLT and a Bolton Corporation ticket machine for use in the appropriate section.

The fleet numbered 71 at its maximum and was notable for the 46 vintage two- and three-axle Roe-bodied Guy trolleybuses. Bought to replace the trams in 1930 and 1931, several were still in use on the day the system ended in 1958. Many were much rebuilt in the early 1950s, it was hard to find two that looked quite the same.

The overhead was erected with due regard to economy. Former tramway bracket arms were often used, span wires were frequently simply tied off round their poles, and there was little use of turn-outs. The vehicles had no traction batteries; their lighting was fed off the overhead supply, dimming on long or loaded sections or going out altogether at section breaks or dewirements.

SLT was a statutory operator established by Act of Parliament and a similar act was needed to wind it up. Because of this and associated financial matters, from 1955 to 1958 fifty five LUT Guy and Daimler double-deckers and Atkinson and Leyland single-deckers were legally owned by SLT.

It all seems very quirky and it was but it worked, carried thousands of passengers and made a profit.

Guy BTX 24 was new in 1931 and ran until the system closed in August 1958. Its Roe body was rebuilt by Bond in the early 1950s with a modernised front end. On the long tortuous route from Farnworth to Atherton, 24 is at Swinton church, where there was a time break and passengers had to rebook. In the background is a Salford Daimler CVG6 on the cross-city 57 with an LUT Dennis Lance on service 20 just appearing on the left of the picture. *1956, Jack Batty*

In Leigh the corporation had its own bus station but most of LUT's services terminated street side in The Avenue whilst SLT had a modest bus station in Spinning Jenny Street. On the right of the picture, still with its original style of front, is Guy BTX 33 bound for Mosley Common colliery. Next to it, going to Bolton, is 1937 Leyland TTB4 53, also Roe-bodied. Bolton Leyland PD2 414 is on the 16 service to Horwich via Atherton and Westhoughton, which also used the SLT station. The 16 was joint with LUT and Leigh but the latter rarely worked it. *February 1956, Jack Batty*

New in 1938, Leyland TTB4 59 leaves Bolton's Howell Croft South bus station for Leigh. In the background is Bolton PD2 81 and two of Bolton's fifteen PD1s with 'dipped window' Crossley bodies. *1956, Jack Batty*

SLT had six wartime Sunbeam W with Weymann bodies to utility standards. Waiting for departure time in Howell Croft South, driver and guard sit in the cab of 61, new in 1943. Like Manchester, LUT referred to its platform staff as 'guards' rather than 'conductors'.*June 1956, Michael Eyre*

Spinning Jenny Street terminus looking towards the street with (above) 1948 Sunbeam MS2 69 departing for Bolton and rebuilt Guy 23 for Mosley Common and (below) 68 also going to Bolton. The six MS2s 66-71, had Weymann bodies and were SLT's only post-war stock; the type could be badged as Sunbeam or a Karrier – to make things more confusing, SLT's were licensed as Sunbeams but had Karrier badges. *1956, Jack Batty*

Leigh

Leigh never operated tramcars and its early buses were garaged in the town's fire station. The fleet outgrew this arrangement and in 1930 a former engineering and ammunitions works in Holden Road was acquired and converted to a garage and workshops. The building's height limit of 13ft 6in restricted the fleet to low-height double-deckers, which mattered little for many years as the town had a number of low railway bridges. These were removed in the 1960s but changes to the garage roof never got beyond the planning stage – something that was to make Leigh the first municipal operator of the Dennis Loline and AEC Renown.

The corporation joined the limited stop bus network in 1928, making additional agreements with LUT, which took the town's buses to Warrington, Wigan and Salford (Manchester on the indicator blinds). Much later it also ran to Bolton, but only after a bitter dispute with LUT over the abandonment of the SLT trolleybuses. During the war the fleet was increased to provide services to the Royal Ordnance factories at Risley, beyond the town's boundaries, and grew to some 60 buses.

Leigh's pre-war preference was for Leylands. It was not swayed by its 13 wartime Guys but after the war there were almost as many AECs as Leylands – 40 of the former and 43 of the latter. There were also half a dozen Dennises.

It was one of the smaller fleets but close to the top of the list for variety.

From 1946 to 1949 Leigh took the unusual step of numbering its new buses downwards from 39 to 4. It also chose some relatively unfamiliar body builders. Eighteen by Charles Roberts of Wakefield were delivered in 1948/49, 36-25 on AEC Regent III chassis and 24-19 on Leyland's PD2. The AECs were withdrawn first – the earliest in 1962 and the last in 1967, the Leylands following in 1966, 1967 and 1968. PD2 21 is in the garage yard with Loline 65 and an AEC Renown in the background.
September 1967, John Kaye

Lydney Coachworks, of the Forest of Dean town of that name, was a subsidiary of the Red and White bus group and rarely built for outside customers. Somehow it was the choice for PD2s 18 to 7 new in 1949/50. By all accounts it was only with substantial rebuilding that the bodies survived into the 1960s – four went in 1964, one in 1966, two in 1968, one in 1969 and four were still in service when SELNEC took over. Number 16 is in Leigh's King Street bus station which was used by corporation services. *August 1969, Roy Marshall*

For all its subsequent bodies Leigh went to East Lancashire Coachbuilders at Blackburn. Delivered in 1952, 40-46 were AEC Regents. A feature of the fleet was the coat of arms transfer at each side of the front indicators; by contrast, the coat of arms was not always applied on the side panels between the words LEIGH and CORPORATION. The ornate red shaded gold lettering and numbers remained a nice feature of Leigh's buses to the end. Here, 44 has just turned off King Street to enter the bus station. *September 1968, Roy Marshall*

The post-war renewal programme completed, there was a gap of three years before more new buses were required. The corporation returned to Leyland for the chassis of its next deliveries – 47-51 in 1955, 52-54 early in 1957 and 55-59 later in that year. Due for overhaul and repaint, 52 leaves the bus station with a full load on the 43 minute journey to Warrington via Glazebury and Winwick, jointly operated with Lancashire United. The Roberts-bodied bus in the background carries a variation of the livery with the fleetname on the cream band although the difference in the blue colour of the two buses is probably due either to variations in paint from different manufacturers or fading, to both of which blue was particularly prone. *August 1963, John Kaye*

The 1957 abandonment of the Bolton–Leigh trolleybus service provoked a major battle between LUT and the corporation when Leigh demanded a share in its operation, LUT stating at one point that it would continue to operate the trolleybuses rather than concede. Compromises were agreed and Leigh got to work one bus on the replacing 82 service. This gave it a problem. LUT would work the 82 with smart new 30ft long highbridge Guy or Leyland double-deckers. Having made a fuss, Leigh's 27ft lowbridge PD2s would not do – it would have to provide something similar and that something would have to fit into Leigh's 13ft 6in high workshops. Thus Leigh became the first municipal operator of the Dennis Loline. Essentially a 30ft Bristol Lodekka built under licence, its dropped-centre rear axle enabled a conventional double-deck layout within Leigh's height restriction. 60/61 arrived in 1958, followed by 62/63 in 1959. All had Gardner 6LW engines and East Lancs rear-entrance bodies. They were also put on the joint 26 service to Salford. 62 is five minutes late with the 4pm departure as it swings out of gloomy Greengate into bright sunshine. *May 1959, John Kaye*

There was something of a throw back to the 1930s in the ogee-shape of the blue paintwork on the side of East Lancs-bodied Leyland Tiger Cubs 1 and 2 delivered in 1960, replacing two 1940 Leyland Tigers. Leigh was one of the few municipal operators with an Act of Parliament that enabled it to operate private hire anywhere beyond its boundaries and the styling and deeper seats reflected this use. *August 1969, Roy Marshall*

Two Mark III Dennis Lolines, 64-65, joined the fleet in 1961. Recognisable by a revised front grille, they had Gardner 6LX engines which would have given a more sparkling on-the-road performance. The fuel tank was placed at the rear end of the rear entrance bus – something of a recipe for trouble in a rear end collision. 64 leaves King Street bus station on service 1 to Plank Lane, where it terminated at Bickershaw Colliery – a large and important mine that closed as recently as 1992. *Summer 1967, Photobus*

The 1962 new vehicles were an extraordinary step backwards. Two 30ft Leyland PD3 chassis with Leigh's usual East Lancs rear-entrance bodies – nothing strange about that. What was almost bizarre was that they were of lowbridge design, with the sunken side gangway and long seats on the upper-deck – and this at a time when, in addition to the Loline, there were low height offerings from AEC (Bridgemaster) and Leyland (Lowlander). Their fleet numbers, 3 and 37, filled gaps in the existing series 1– 65. *August 1968, Roy Marshall*

In 1963 Leigh was the first to get AEC's new low-height Renown chassis – sharing the honour with South Wales Transport. 25-28 were the first for a municipal operator and the only Renowns with rear-entrance bodies (East Lancs, of course). 25 has just passed the Eagle and Child pub in Twist Lane en route to Plank Lane. *April 1969, Geoffrey Morant*

Fourteen more Renowns followed over the years 1964 to 1967 and they had front entrances. Like the PD3s, their fleet numbers filled vacant gaps. Its paintwork looking somewhat tired in the pale sunshine, 5 leaves Greengate, Salford on limited stop service 26 back to its home town. *Summer 1969, Photobus*

The last new Leigh Corporation buses were five Leyland Leopard/East Lancs single-deckers fitted for one-man operation. They were painted in a revised livery yet retained the splendid gold numbers and lettering. Number 20 was two-man operated on this journey on LUT joint service 48 to Lane Head through Pennington and Lowton, which passed the former site of Cowley's used bus yard. *May 1969, Geoffrey Morant*

Wigan

Wigan's fleet of about 150 was perhaps the best example of a Lancashire municipal transport department – Leyland chassis, bodies built in Lancashire, a maroon and white livery, ornate gold shaded fleet numbers and lettering, plus a few eccentricities. Fleet numbering was one of these – new buses were given, more or less randomly, numbers left vacant by withdrawn buses and only when gaps had been filled was the sequence extended.

Another quirk of the Wigan fleet was the pair of green lights on either side of the front indicators. Originally prompted by the vaguely similar colour of the Ribble buses in the town, their purpose was to identify a corporation bus at night so that passengers would use it rather than a Ribble. Introduced in the 1920s, the lights continued to be fitted to the end of the transport department's existence in 1974.

In transport terms Wigan was on the edge of what became Greater Manchester and the limited stop bus network scarcely affected the corporation's services. Its buses worked to Bolton and Liverpool but not on service 32 to Manchester, although it was nominally a joint operator. In addition to the corporation's fleet, there were Ribble and LUT buses and whatever was in work at bus body builders Northern Counties, in Wigan Lane to the north of the town centre, and Massey Brothers in Pemberton to the south-west. There was a lot to see at Wigan.

For its post-war fleet renewal Wigan bought large batches of Leylands. Rather than supporting local industry at Northern Counties and Massey Brothers, both based in the town, the body contract also went to Leyland and there are many stories as to why. That said, it was a good choice. In 1946/7 there were seventy five lowbridge PD1s – like Leigh, Wigan had several low railway bridges. They were withdrawn over a prolonged period – the first went in 1959. One of the last was 83, still in fine condition in June 1966 waiting in Market Place to turn into Library Street. It was sold in March 1967. *June 1966, Geoffrey Morant*

The PD1s were followed in 1950 by thirty Leyland PD2s. Also with Leyland bodies they were Wigan's first highbridge buses. Taken at the same point a few minutes after the previous shot, 152 was sold just over a year after 83. The circular green lights on either side of the front indicators show nicely on this picture. Lancashire United had something similar on its buses. Up to 1950 there were three tiny white lights above or below the front indicators – they can be clearly seen on the pictures of LUT 362 and 436 in this book. *June 1966, Geoffrey Morant*

Twelve more Leyland-bodied PD2s joined the fleet in 1953. On Wallgate, 98 has just passed the splendid cast iron forecourt canopy of Wallgate railway station. Although most Wigan Corporation services were shown as starting in the town centre, several were linked to give cross-town running – for example 23 (Worsley Hall) was linked to service 12 (Abram), hence the 'via Wigan' on 98's indicator, the bus having come from Abram. *September 1968, Roy Marshall*

Wigan's single-deck fleet included four Leyland Royal Tigers new in 1951, four more in 1953, one in 1955 and two Tiger Cubs in 1957. All had Northern Counties bodies of that firm's standard design. Above is 82, one of the 1951 Royal Tigers. *June 1966, Geoffrey Morant*

Below is Tiger Cub 104 in the parking area of Wigan bus station, surrounded by three Ribble Leylands and an LUT Guy. Service 333/343 to Wrightington and its famous orthopaedic hospital was worked jointly with Ribble and had a Ribble number. *September 1968, Roy Marshall*

Leyland's sudden decision to stop building bus bodies was good news for Wigan's two bus builders and the corporation's future business was divided between the two, more or less in proportion to their size. Ten Leyland PD3s were delivered in 1959, six with Northern Counties bodies and four with Massey, of which number 60 was one. This is the classic Massey design and it was very well built and equally nicely finished. *September 1968, Roy Marshall*

Later deliveries were the Leyland PD3A model – the 'A' signifying the 'St Helens' engine cowl. This is 77, one of nine delivered in late 1962 – five with Massey bodies and the other four, including 77 bodied by Northern Counties. The X suffix to the service number indicates a short working to Newtown, not far from the town centre. *June 1966, Geoffrey Morant*

An offside shot of the Massey body. Wigan 6, pictured here at Martland Mill terminus, was one of three Massey-bodied Leyland PD3s new in 1957 – the others were numbered 2 and 4. Enjoying the break between arrival and departure, the crew sit facing each other on the longitudinal seats over the rear wheel arches in the lower deck. Wigan is a rugby town and they are likely to be chatting about the coming rugby league match against Yorkshire rivals Bramley – a paper advertising the match is behind the seat back. *Roy Marshall, October 1962*

The Massey body on 1962 Leyland Tiger Cub 21 was very plain and angular. En route to Orrell Post on a 20 from Standish, 21 is at Gathurst passing under the former Lancashire & Yorkshire railway line from Manchester to Southport. The place is not as quiet as it may seem – the contractor's signs on the left of the picture are for works associated with the construction of the M6 Gathurst viaduct a few hundred yards to the left. The bridges over the River Douglas and Leeds Liverpool canal can be seen through the arch of the railway bridge. *March 1963, Roy Marshall*

Besides corporation buses, you would see plenty of Ribble buses in Wigan. Its garage in the town had an allocation of about 45. Ribble Atlantean 1646 bound for Southport is passing Wigan 56, a 1963 Northern Counties-bodied PD2A with the so-called St Helens style of front cowl, loading for Bryn on service 2. The batch was twelve – six with Massey bodies (fleet numbers 41, 43-45, 47/48) and six with Northern Counties (52, 55, 56, 69, 75, 76). *June 1966, Geoffrey Morant*

Single-deck Massey bodies were uncommon. In 1967 Wigan took two on Leyland Panther Cub chassis. The styling was neat enough, using the BET-group's style of front and rear, although Wigan's maroon-painted rear dome looked odd. Number 20, new in July 1967, is outside the corporation's fine modern garage in Melverley Street, a few hundred yards from the town centre. *August 1968, Roy Marshall*

Massey was run by Arthur Tyldesley who liked to pick his clients and what he built for them – and he could: 'best bodies ever' said one general manager. With the market for traditional vehicles declining, the firm was sold to Northern Counties in 1967. Wigan's last Massey-bodied buses, part finished by Northern Counties, arrived in 1968 by which time the firm's half cab design had also evolved to a square look. Outside Wigan's Olympic-size swimming pool, six month-old number 32 turns from Library Street into Rodney Street. *September 1968, Roy Marshall*

With local pride, Northern Counties would often put a local bus on its stand at the Commercial Motor Show and it would be finished to a very high standard. For its 1969 deliveries Wigan ordered its first Atlanteans and one was an obvious choice, so much so that it was completed ready for the show in September 1968, six months ahead of the other nine. Here it is outside the garage, its polished paintwork gleaming. Amongst its special details were a small blue and silver British Leyland badge above the number plate and a registration number, FJP 566G, that went with its fleet number 166. *October 1968, Roy Marshall*

In surroundings very typical of the outskirts of the borough and, indeed of the Lancashire coalfield, 161 of the same batch is on the A573 Warrington Road near the junction of Cemetery Road between Ince and Platt Bridge. *Summer 1969, Photobus*

The corporation's 1970 delivery was of twelve Leyland 36ft-long rear-engined Panthers with Northern Counties high capacity bodies – 46 seated, 21 standing. They were numbered in one block, 80-91. This is 88 outside the Market Hall and the bus station on a grey overcast June day in 1971. The driver is wearing his lightweight summer uniform jacket. *June 1971, Roy Marshall*

Twelve Atlanteans in 1971, numbered 92-97, 151-156, were followed by ten more in 1972. Numbered 1-10, they were the corporation's last new buses. By that time SELNEC's standard double-decker was in production at Northern Counties and these used its frame and layout but with traditional details. The two green lights were still fitted but the shaded fleet number transfers had been replaced by something more plain. Number 5 on Pottery Road, bound for Windy Arbour colliery. *March 1973, Roy Marshall*